# Reading and Preaching the
# BOOK OF ISAIAH

# Reading and Preaching the
# BOOK OF ISAIAH

**CHRISTOPHER R. SEITZ**
*editor*

FORTRESS PRESS            PHILADELPHIA

---

**Library of Congress Cataloging-in-Publication Data**

Reading and preaching the Book of Isaiah.

    1. Bible. O.T. Isaiah—Criticism, interpretation, etc. I. Seitz, Christopher R.
BS1515.2.R43   1988   224′.106       86-46432
ISBN 0-8006-2056-9

---

Printed in the United States of America           1-2056

95   94   93   92   91      2   3   4   5   6   7   8   9   10

# Contents

# Contributors

ELIZABETH ACHTEMEIER
Professor of Bible and Homiletics
Union Theological Seminary in Virginia

JAMES LUTHER MAYS
Professor of Hebrew and Old Testament
Union Theological Seminary in Virginia

ROBERT R. WILSON
Professor of Old Testament
Yale University, The Divinity School

WALTER BRUEGGEMANN
Professor of Old Testament
Columbia Theological Seminary

PAUL D. HANSON
Professor of Old Testament
Harvard University, The Divinity School

CHRISTOPHER R. SEITZ
Associate Professor of Old Testament
Yale University, The Divinity School

# Preface

A word is in order concerning the evolution of this book. The core of the book (chaps. 1–6) consists of a series of lectures delivered at the Lutheran Theological Seminary at Philadelphia in the spring of 1986. The speakers were asked to prepare lectures on the Book of Isaiah for an audience composed of seminarians, local clergy, and the interested public.

In planning a series such as this, several possibilities for organization (thematic, historical, literary) were suggested. In this century, of course, almost every approach to Isaiah has worked with the theory that the Book of Isaiah consists of at least three major collections: First Isaiah (chaps. 1—39); Second or Deutero-Isaiah (chaps. 40—55); and Third Isaiah (chaps. 56—66). We saw no reason for moving away from this helpful and, if nothing else, practical way of dividing the book. It solved part of the problem of how to set up the series and distribute lecture assignments. Accordingly, we sought the best speakers available for each of the respective sections of the book. The reader of this volume should agree that we found them.

With this familiar method of approach in place, it also seemed desirable in concluding the series to see if we might make something out of the Isaiah corpus as a literary whole. Several excellent attempts have been made in recent years to address this very question: Is there a way to interpret the sixty-six-chapter Book of Isaiah as a literary and theological unity? Not knowing exactly what would result, I agreed to lecture on this final topic. This presentation of the Book of Isaiah, therefore, includes two essays on Isaiah 1—39, two on Isaiah 40—55, and one on Isaiah 56—66, together with my final commentary on reading Isaiah as a sixty-six-chapter work.

One other item of interest—and acknowledgment—is necessary at this point. As the series took place in the spring of 1986, I discovered that I had one advantage no one else participating in the Three-Isaiah format had. I was the only lecturer in the series who had the pleasure of hearing all the other lecturers. By the time I was due to present my own lecture, the contents of the entire Book of Isaiah had been admirably reviewed for me, thus making my summary task much easier. But more importantly, my role as host speaker meant that I could review the problems associated with the traditional or the newer holistic models of interpretation. Moreover, I could discuss these problems, and possible solutions, with each of the individual speakers in turn. I learned much in this exchange, and want to acknowledge with gratitude the helpful conversation I was able to have with each of the five speakers, whose essays precede my own in this volume, *Reading and Preaching the Book of Isaiah*.

It is of course one thing to benefit from an exciting and challenging lecture series, and quite another thing to place the contents of that series in book format. However, in discussing the possibility of a book with Fortress Press editors, it became obvious to all of us that these lectures would profitably form the backbone of a volume on the Book of Isaiah. Much of the oral form of the original lectures has been carried over into the essays as they appear in this volume. The result is a style that makes for lively and engaging reading.

Three particular strengths of the series—even better seen in the present format—bear notice. First, the speakers are without exception acknowledged Old Testament scholars, and experts in their field. As such, this volume does a superb job of acquainting the general reader with critical problems associated with interpreting, preaching, or just simply reading any biblical book. At the same time, the reader will note the way in which theological issues raised by a sensitive reading of the Book of Isaiah are boldly and creatively engaged by the authors. Isaiah's word is no historic artifact, but a lively and relentless challenge to the modern world. These essays raise many new possibilities for reading and preaching. Finally, *Reading and Preaching the Book of Isaiah* attempts to bring the reader into dialogue with the most recent trends in Isaiah interpretation. While the book operates with the familiar tradition-historical model of interpretation, it contains within it a reflection on the strengths and weaknesses of this model of approach. Something of the force of recent critical moves is sketched out in the introduction that follows. A full treatment appears in my essay "Isaiah 1—66: Making Sense of the Whole," which concludes this volume.

For those wishing to use this book in the context of Bible study or adult discussion, note that the videotapes of the original lecture series are now available through *Select*. For information, contact Norman Wegmeyer, Trinity Lutheran Seminary, 2199 E. Main Street, Columbus, OH 43209. The video format is now helpfully enhanced by this volume, which provides as well an introduction to the critical background from which the lectures emerged.

A volume such as this cannot appear without the help and cooperation of many people. To Timothy Lull, who encouraged us at the Lutheran Theological Seminary at Philadelphia to engage in biblical study as a whole seminary, and to those who assisted with the Spring 1986 Biblical Emphasis Symposium, thanks are certainly in order. More directly, I would like to thank the speakers in the series for their original work. Enthusiasm for the series has clearly spilled over into this project. For the extra effort that helped transform lectures into book chapters, and for bits of advice about the overall format of the book, I can only thank the speakers as a whole. It is a reward in itself to be included among such a lively and challenging group of scholars.

A final word of gratitude must be extended to John A. Hollar at Fortress Press. His customary candor, good will, and good sense were at every juncture appreciated. The book owes much to his enthusiasm and encouragement.

CHRISTOPHER R. SEITZ
Philadelphia, Pa.

# Introduction:
# The One Isaiah //
# The Three Isaiahs

CHRISTOPHER R. SEITZ

## Dividing Prophetic Books

In modern commentaries on individual biblical books, the work under investigation is frequently divided into smaller sections. This is especially true of commentaries on the larger prophetic collections. While a single volume might suffice for the nine-chapter Book of Amos, the same is not true for the more expansive works of Isaiah, Jeremiah, and Ezekiel.

Rough and ready divisions are not always apparent in these larger prophetic books. Sometimes the internal literary evidence is strong in favor of dividing in a certain way. So, for example, Jeremiah frequently appears in the form of two volumes, divided into chapters 1—25 and chapters 26—45/52.[1] On other occasions, decisions about where to begin and end separate volumes appear to be governed by more practical considerations. So it is, for example, that Ezekiel is divided in the Hermeneia commentary series into chapters 1—24 (vol. 1) and chapters 25—48 (vol. 2). In the first volume to appear in the Anchor Bible series, Moshe Greenberg has found some logic in treating chapters 1—20 of Ezekiel as a workable unit.[2] In either case arguments could be mounted for the appropriateness of the respective dividing points, but in both cases the result is the same: the Book of Ezekiel appears in two volumes of roughly equal length.

By contrast, considerations governing the subdivision of the Book of Isaiah are of an altogether different order. Here sensible literary arguments and practical concerns play a certain role. But final judgment must in the end defer to what is in many ways the greatest historical-critical consensus of the modern period: the division of Isaiah 1—66 into the two or three Isaiahs represented by chapters 1—39, 40—55, and 56—66. Practical and literary concerns now inform the dividing of Isaiah 1—39 into yet smaller volumes. But here we have already moved into a situation where the concept of First Isaiah is so firmly fixed that even a reduced corpus of thirty-nine chapters (lacking 40—66) must itself be further subdivided, along the analogy of an Ezekiel or Jeremiah!

Similarly, because modern introductions to the Old Testament generally follow a historical outline, First Isaiah is introduced to the reader with the other Assyrian period prophets: Amos, Hosea, and Micah. Discussion of Isaiah 40—55 is then postponed until Jeremiah and Ezekiel, and perhaps Lamentations, have been properly surveyed. The corpus of the Second Isaiah is taken to be extensive and independent enough to warrant attempts at a life sketch of the prophet—even ones that despair over the lack of biographical detail in chapters 40—55. Second Isaiah is not only treated as a free-standing literary work and prophetic figure in standard introductions, but he is also the subject of several book-length studies.[3] Similar circumstances obtain for Trito-Isaiah and chapters 56—66.[4]

Charles C. Torrey, who argued in a different day for a different division of the larger Book of Isaiah, opined that the term "Deutero-Isaiah" ought to be replaced by the simpler "Second Isaiah" for the benefit of the astute, less educated but omnipresent "man in the pew."[5] He would be surprised or irritated to discover that the terms are now used almost interchangeably. Moreover, so wide a consensus exists for the validity of the Three-Isaiah model that it is a rare student or layperson who has not come across the terms "Deutero-" or even "Trito-" Isaiah as the very first among the initiatory rites of modern biblical interpretation.

All this suggests that when we move to a discussion of the Book of Isaiah, we have moved onto a very different plane. It appears that with the Book of Isaiah we have at last found one of those cases where "the assured results of critical scholarship" are in fact assured. A critical tenet, promoted and then fiercely debated not many years ago, has now become the standard point of entry into the world of Isaiah. And unlike other, perhaps more complex, critical theories, the Three-Isaiah theory has moved from the realm of university/seminary discussion into general parlance.

Again it is helpful to contrast Isaiah's canonical neighbors Jeremiah and Ezekiel. One could argue that something of a growing consensus exists about secondary or tertiary levels within the books of Jeremiah and Ezekiel. But an important and purely practical distinction exists. It is most unlikely that a separate commentary will ever appear on the "deuteronomistic redaction" of the Book of Jeremiah, even though, like Second Isaiah, this represents a new and tolerably coherent layer of Jeremiah tradition. Individual chapters within standard Old Testament introductions might risk a separate treatment of Ezekiel's program of restoration (chaps. 40—48). But this kind of literary separation only roughly mirrors the situation as we find it in the Book of Isaiah. New strata are not as easily blocked off in Ezekiel or Jeremiah on historical, literary, or theological grounds.

The telling feature of the Book of Isaiah is that, from a critical as well as a practical standpoint, the sixty-six chapters give the impression of growing coherently, beginning at the beginning, middling at the middle, and ending at the end. It looks as though Isaiah is a library or anthology—so it has been described—which grew by means of simple expansion: chapters 1—39 "updated" by chapters 40—55, themselves filled out by chapters 56—66.[6] All of this happened, it seems, according to a coherent historical unfolding. The first chapters came from the first (Assyrian) period, the second from the second (Babylonian), the third from the third (Persian). And there is no pattern quite like this in the other major prophetic collections.

This apparently coherent growth pattern has meant that Isaiah can be practically packaged under the titles "First Isaiah," "Second Isaiah," and "Third Isaiah." Separate commentary volumes, chapters in critical introductions, or specialized studies can proceed with this handy division as a starting point. The same will not work for Ezekiel or Jeremiah. Staying with this observation a bit longer, one further feature about the Book of Isaiah is to be noted, namely, its breadth of historical coverage. Ranging over three separate historical epochs as it does (Assyrian, Babylonian, Persian), correct interpretation of the sixty-six-chapter Isaiah would seem to demand tripartite division. Here again, the notion that this division corresponds to separate literary sections of the book is both attractive and convenient. And because the historical range of the book is as long as it is, moving well beyond the lifetime of the historical Isaiah ben Amoz (Isa. 1:1), new prophetic personalities would appear to be demanded as an explanation for the literary expansions represented by chapters 40—55 and 56—66. Hence, the decision in nearly all quarters to deal with the one Book of Isaiah as Three Isaiahs.

I rehearse this unfolding of critical theory again in order to emphasize the extent to which the "Three Isaiahs" have found their place within any modern discussion of the Book of Isaiah. Practical, literary, and theological reasons all converge in support of this critical approach. A critical model of relatively recent vintage is seen as offering the single most important, if not indispensable, lens through which we view the sixty-six-chapter Book of Isaiah. And it provides the framework for the presentation of Isaiah in the chapters that follow.

## The Critical Emergence of Three Isaiahs

To compare a contemporary reading of the Book of Isaiah with one done just a hundred years ago is to go on an interesting journey. It was not just that distinctions of style and substance, such as undergird the modern tripartite division, had gone unnoticed. So-called precritical readers recognized a marked change of style and background when the boundary of chapter 40 was crossed. But these changes in style were viewed as going hand in hand with the subject matter related by the prophet Isaiah.[7] Isaiah had spoken of judgment, but now he spoke of restoration. Certainly, a change in tone and imagery could be expected when this shift in subject matter occurred. The net effect required little strain on the reader's imagination.

When the back of opposition to the modern critical approach was broken, the toughest hurdle to be overcome proved not to be the specifics of the Three-Isaiah theory, but rather far more general considerations. These involved fundamental notions of how the Old Testament prophets were to be conceived. To deny the eighth-century prophet Isaiah the ability to foresee and dramatically depict Israel's restoration at the hands of Yahweh was to strike at the root of basic understandings of prophecy and the nature of Old Testament literature itself. Tampering with this could only threaten larger theological assumptions. It was not just the predictive capability of the prophet that was being impugned.[8] Even the more conservative position was not anxious to encourage an overly "supernatural" view of prophecy, one that in the end might promote a bizarre or exotic conception of the biblical prophets.[9]

Looking at the debates with one hundred years of hindsight, what seemed of crucial importance was the veracity of the literature itself, and its ability to speak simply and truthfully about its contents. We are told by the Book of Isaiah that it consists of a "vision of Isaiah, son of Amoz, which he saw concerning Judah and Jerusalem," in the days of four eighth-century Judahite kings (Isa. 1:1). To say otherwise was not just to spin more-or-less believable yarns about the Book of Isaiah, its growth and development. It was to call into question the literature's ability to speak directly and coherently to the reader *on its own terms.*[10] Once critical judgment was able to operate with principles external to the literature itself, defense of the older view began to look strained, idiosyncratic, and suspiciously defensive. In the interim, an altogether different understanding of prophecy had emerged. To use a phrase popular in the period, the prophets were now to be thought of not as "foretellers" but as "forth-tellers." The result was a major shift in the way the biblical prophets were to be conceived. In turn, straightforward reading of the prophetic literature was radically affected, as was the proclamation of the prophet's word to the present community of faith.[11]

In the twentieth century, the external principles necessary for historical analysis of the prophetic books have been refined to the most precise degree. There can be no nostalgic return to a unified Isaiah, as was argued for in the late nineteenth century. This notion of unity had depended upon the conviction that sole authorship of the sixty-six-chapter corpus was accomplished by the eighth-century Isaiah. Unity of message demanded a consistent authorial voice. There may be newer critical attempts to describe the literary and editorial features that enable us to read a highly complex, multilayered Book of Isaiah as a unified whole. But these modern studies already assume that the unity, or coherence, of the whole Book of Isaiah is a feature that does not require single authorship by the prophet Isaiah. Unity and coherence are sought rather in the "reciprocal relationships" between the literary blocks of First (1—39), Second (40—55), and Third (56—66) Isaiah.[12]

With respect to the general notion of three basic blocks of Isaianic material, critical findings of this century have proven relatively solid.

Ironically, it could be said that the recent search for unity and coherence in the Book of Isaiah, along literary and theological lines, has become a concern of the newer redaction-critical studies precisely because it is now taken as settled that the message of the larger book has moved far beyond the original eighth-century setting of the historical Isaiah. The question now to be asked is: What are the internal literary features that enable us to read this multilayered collection as a coherent whole?

Once serious defense of single authorship for the Book of Isaiah was relegated to the periphery of modern biblical studies, the actual historical setting of the oracles of the Book of Isaiah could be explored more fully. On the whole, the Three-Isaiah model has here proven helpful. It remains an excellent way to enter the literary corpus of a sixty-six-chapter Isaiah, even when its shortcomings are acknowledged. Chief among these, for example, is the notion of a unified First Isaiah corpus, which corresponds to chapters 1—39 and is traceable to the prophet Isaiah ben Amoz.[13] In fact, the First Isaiah corpus contains material from the most diverse historical periods, ranging from the eighth through at least the sixth century.

Even granting modifications, the significance of a model of growth that understands the book evolving through three major periods is to be upheld. At the same time, the newer redactional studies of Isaiah have raised many fresh and challenging insights into the growth of the Isaianic collection. In a strict sense, use of the term First Isaiah to describe chapters 1—39 must be qualified in light of the fact that much material in these chapters actually postdates Second Isaiah or even Third Isaiah chapters. An additive process of growth, governed by purely historical factors, misunderstands the nature of prophecy generally, and the Book of Isaiah specifically, a work one recent commentator called "one of the most complex literary structures in the entire Old Testament."[14] What remains as an essential task is a clearer description of the intention behind the merger of these various literary strata, the result being our present Book of Isaiah.

## Reading and Preaching Isaiah

In the chapters that follow, the Three-Isaiah model provides the critical means by which the message of the entire book is explored. Especially in seeking to interpret and proclaim the prophets' word to a modern audience, it is helpful to begin with the more workable literary units set forth as the Three Isaiahs. There are several reasons for this. *Preaching* the biblical prophets demands close attention to the historical age in which the message was delivered.[15] With a clearer understanding of the circumstances under which the prophetic word first went forth, the preacher is better equipped to make modern applications. The prophetic word is not a timeless truth, uttered in isolation from the concrete events of history. As such, all modern application of that word must take seriously its time-conditioned quality and the circumstances under which it was proclaimed. In the case of the Book of Isaiah, three basic historical situations can be reconstructed: (1) for (much of) chapters 1—39: Judah in the Assyrian period, especially during the critical years of Ahaz and Hezekiah; (2) for chapters 40—55: Israel in exile, in the mid–sixth century B.C.E., during the period of waning Babylonian strength; and (3) for chapters 56—66: Judah/Jerusalem in the late sixth century, back in the homeland, concerned with the reestablishment of the community along social and religious lines.

*Reading* the whole Book of Isaiah involves a similar measure of imagination. The prophetic literature has across every age produced a variety of responses, many of simple bewilderment.[16] With the Three-Isaiah model in place as an aid to interpretation of the book's entire message, it requires a suspension of strictly historical-critical interest to try and read the sixty-six-chapter book as a coherent literary and theological composition. And yet such a reading is not only desirable, but also demanded, once it is assumed that part of the intention behind the present growth of the tradition was not merely the result of accident or historical expedient. There are good reasons for defending the view that the Book of Isaiah received its present form through a set of complex literary arrangements, whose purpose was to make the present book intelligible as a whole product to future generations, who would seek therein a coherent Word of God based upon this great—even sixty-six-chapter—vision of Isaiah. Before this line of inquiry can be pursued in more detail, the Three Isaiahs must be allowed their respective say.

History and theology and literary complexity are three features that cannot be treated in isolation when one seeks to read and preach the Book of Isaiah. As has been noted, there is a danger in dismissing the historical world in which this complex literary message was given birth.

Yet at the same time, the original oral message was not left behind to speak a restricted word to generations now long gone. The production of prophetic literature, especially fuller prophetic collections such as the Book of Isaiah, involves factors not entirely clear to the modern reader, and understanding the present shape of the Book of Isaiah is no easy task. At every juncture the reader is aware that here we have a literature without clear modern analogy. But it can be assumed at a minimum that even as the oral word went forth, at the point in time when the historical prophet was recognized as an authentic spokesman for Israel's only Lord, there was a desire to enshrine that word in coherent literary form, that it might address generations yet unborn (Isa. 8:16–22). This was true not only for the original word proclaimed by Isaiah of Jerusalem, in the mid–eighth century, but also for the many words which emerged at later moments in history, forming a wider sixty-six-chapter corpus, described as a whole product by later generations: "The vision of Isaiah the son of Amoz which he saw concerning Judah and Jerusalem" (Isa. 1:1).

It is only with these historical and literary considerations in place that the rich theological message of the sixty-six-chapter book can sound again for the present community of faith. In interpreting the prophetic message, attention must be paid to both historical and literary contexts. In Isaiah these contexts involve not just three centuries of events in the life of Israel and God, but also a full sixty-six-chapter literary panorama. The strength of the present volume, *Reading and Preaching the Book of Isaiah,* is precisely that the possible tension between the historical and literary contexts is never fully resolved. Both perspectives commend themselves to the sensitive reader and preacher of Isaiah. In this one sense, the threefold presentation of Isaiah in the following chapters is itself far more than the result of practical accommodation or mere convenience. As the reader moves through the historical world of three Isaiahs and three Israels in three distinct periods, the question of unity and coherence in the sixty-six-chapter book is not set aside. For ultimately the unity of the Book of Isaiah is not to be sought in issues of single authorship or uniform historical setting, but rather in the common witness of all sixty-six chapters to the one God of Israel, Isaiah's "Holy One," who casts down and raises up, whose justice shapes the cosmos itself, and whose promises extend into a future beyond the horizon of the book's own historical and literary world. In the complex literary, historical, and theological "vision of Isaiah," a drama unfolds that captures the imagination, while at the same instant revealing the eternal purpose of the one God with whom we have to do.

> Remember this and consider, recall it to mind, you transgressors, remember the former things of old; for I am God, and there is no other; I am God, and there is none like me, declaring the end from the beginning and from ancient times things not yet done, saying, "My counsel shall stand, and I will accomplish all my purpose." I have spoken, and I will bring it to pass; I have purposed, and I will do it. (Isa. 46:8-11)

## NOTES

1. For Jeremiah, see Cambridge Commentary on the New English Bible (E.W. Nicholson); International Critical Commentary (William McKane); Neue Echter Bibel (J. Schreiner); Hermeneia (William Holladay). Also, in his recent critical monograph, *Die deuteronomistische Redaktion von Jeremia*, W. Thiel has divided Jeremiah at chaps. 1—25 (Wissenschaftliche Monographien zum Alten und Neuen Testament 41 [Neukirchen-Vluyn: Neukirchner, 1973]); and chaps. 26—45 (Wissenschaftliche Monographien zum Alten und Neuen Testament 52 [Neukirchen-Vluyn: Neukirchner, 1981]).

2. See Greenberg's interesting discussion of the traditional "tannaitic bipartition" of Ezekiel into dooms and consolations, thought to imply the division followed by many at 1—24 and 25—48 (*Ezekiel 1—20*, Anchor Bible 22 [New York: Doubleday & Co., 1983], 3-6).

3. James D. Smart, *History and Theology in Second Isaiah* (Philadelphia: Westminster Press, 1965); George A. F. Knight, *Deutero-Isaiah: A Theological Commentary on Isaiah 40—55* (Nashville: Abingdon Press, 1965); Christopher R. North, *The Second Isaiah* (Oxford: At the Clarendon Press, 1964).

4. K. Elliger, *Die Einheit Tritojesajas* (Stuttgart: Kohlhammer, 1928); Elizabeth Achtemeier, *The Community and Message of Isaiah 56—66* (Minneapolis: Augsburg Pub. House, 1982). Achtemeier prefers corporate authorship by prophets in "the Isaianic school of 538-515 B.C." who "understood themselves as members of an elect community that had taken over the role of the Suffering Servant of Second Isaiah" (16).

5. C.C. Torrey, *The Second Isaiah: A New Interpretation* (New York: Charles Scribner's Sons, 1928), 3.

6. See, e.g., the judgment of Robert Pfeiffer, who could state with utter assurance and simplicity: "Anonymous prophecies in Isa. 40—66 filled up the space left on the first scroll after the Book of Isaiah [i.e., chaps. 1—39] was copied" (*Introduction to the Old Testament*, rev. ed. [New York: Harper & Brothers, 1948], 415).

7. In defense of the traditional position, Karl Friedrich Keil admitted: "It is

impossible to avoid noticing that the representation in ch. xl.—lxvi. on the whole has greater clearness, transparency, ease, fluency, copiousness, and breadth, than the acknowledged genuine discourses in the first part." He then went on to conclude: "But this diversity is perfectly explained by the diversity in the object handled" (*Manual of Historico-Critical Introduction to the Canonical Scriptures of the Old Testament* [Edinburgh: T. & T. Clark, 1892], 1:329).

8. This capability seems to be assumed as early as the first century B.C.E. in Jesus ben Sira: "With a spirit of power he [Isaiah] saw the future and he comforted the mourners of Zion, To the end of time he showed things to be, and hidden things before their coming" (Ecclus. 48:24-25).

9. Or, one that turned the prophets into mechanistic prognosticators. Again, it is helpful to read Keil's arguments carefully. It is important for him that Isaiah's vision of the future remain somewhat shadowy ("according to certain general ideas," *Manual of Historico-Critical Introduction*, 324). Concerning the prophet's specific naming of Cyrus at Isa. 44:28 and 45:1, Keil responds: "[Cyrus] is surely mentioned: yet he is not depicted as the king of Persia, in the manner of his appearance in history, but is predicted in thoroughly ideal lineaments" (324).

10. What Hans Frei calls the text's explicative sense, as against its historical (meaning-as-reference) sense (*The Eclipse of Biblical Narrative* [New Haven, Conn.: Yale Univ. Press, 1974]).

11. As Brevard Childs has put it, "The hermeneutical principle became virtually axiomatic that a biblical book could only be properly understood when interpreted in light of its original historical setting" (*Introduction to the Old Testament as Scripture* [Philadelphia: Fortress Press, 1979], 317).

12. This useful expression appears (in English translation) in Rolf Rendtorff's recent *The Old Testament: An Introduction* (Philadelphia: Fortress Press, 1986), 190-200. See also his "Zur Komposition des Buches Jesaja," *Vetus Testamentum* 34 (1984): 295-320. Ronald Clements refers to the "truly intrinsic connection of content between the various blocks of material" ("Beyond Tradition-History: Deutero-Isaianic Development of First Isaiah's Themes," *Journal for the Study of the Old Testament* 31 [1985]: 97).

13. Suggested, e.g., in Pfeiffer's statement in n. 6 above.

14. Clements, "Beyond Tradition-History," 98.

15. Elizabeth Achtemeier, author of the opening chapter on First Isaiah, offers a clear statement of the benefit of historical analysis in her treatment of Third Isaiah. See *Community and Message of Isaiah 56-66,* 9-11.

16. On confronting the prophet's message, Luther stated, "They [the prophets] have a queer way of talking, like people who, instead of proceeding in an orderly manner, ramble off from one thing to the next, so that you cannot make head or tail of them or see what they are getting at" (quoted from Gerhard von Rad, *The Message of the Prophets* [New York: Harper & Row, 1967], 15).

# 1

# Isaiah of Jerusalem: Themes and Preaching Possibilities

## ELIZABETH ACHTEMEIER

### Introduction and Background

Isaiah's book is one of the four books of the Old Testament most frequently quoted in the New Testament, and for that reason alone it is of great importance to us. However, that is by no means the only reason why the book has value for us or why it has played so prominent a role in the life of the church. Isaiah of Jerusalem is one of the greatest theologians in the Old Testament, and in the midst of his turbulent world, he sets forth distinctive witnesses to the person and activity of God that persist and influence all the rest of the biblical canon. At the same time, Isaiah marks a watershed in the history of Israel. The prophet's ministry covers the period from 742 to 701 B.C.E., and during that time an age ends in Israel's life and an age begins. When King Ahaz of Judah summons the empire of Assyria to his aid during the Syro-Ephraimitic war, in 735 B.C.E., Israel loses her political independence, and does not regain it again until a brief time under the Maccabees, in the second century B.C.E. (165–143), and then not again until the creation by the United Nations of the modern Israeli state in 1948. It is given to Isaiah to interpret that sea change in Israel's fortunes.

As for the man himself, as is the case with all of the prophets except Jeremiah, we do not know very much about him—these prophets' personal biographies have value only in the service of God. We do know that Isaiah is rather unique among the prophets in that he is a city man, apparently born, raised, bred, and married in Jerusalem. He may have even been nobly born—he is the son of one Amoz—and Talmudic tradition (Meg. 10b) holds that Amoz was the brother of King Amaziah of Judah (800–783 B.C.E.). Certainly Isaiah has free access, without being summoned, to the kings of his state (7:1–14), and he acts as a counselor to Hezekiah (37:1–7). We are dealing with the upper class when we deal with the Book of Isaiah—and that seems to me a comforting assurance that even we well-to-do Americans can serve our Lord. Not surprisingly, however, it is against his own wealthy compatriots that Isaiah often levels God's judgments, and that is a phenomenon not found too often in our wealthier churches.

For example, if one reads the judgment oracles against the rich women of Jerusalem, in 3:16–26, the description could match that of a fashion model straight out of any modern women's magazine. Isaiah describes the women of his time as having pendants and bracelets and scarves, perfume boxes and handbags, well-set hair and garments of gauze and linen. They are haughty, says the prophet, "and walk with outstretched necks, glancing wantonly with their eyes, mincing along as they go." Or for another example, the woe oracles of the prophet, in chapter 5 of his book, could fit the characters we watch every week on the television show "Dallas."

> Woe to those who join house to house,
>    who add field to field,
> until there is no more room,
>    and you are made to dwell alone
> in the midst of the land. (Isa. 5:8)

> Woe to those who are heroes at drinking wine,
>    and valiant men in mixing strong drink,
> who acquit the guilty for a bribe,
>    and deprive the innocent of his right! (Isa. 5:22–23)

This book is very pertinent, in its setting and accusations, to the society in which we live. Isaiah too has sons, though they are not J. R. and Bobby, but Shearjashub ("a remnant shall return") and Maher-shalal-hash-baz ("the spoil speeds, the prey hastes"), and we could profit from knowing what those names mean.

At any rate, we are moving in an urban world in the Book of Isaiah, a world where agriculture, with its concerns for fertility, does not play a prominent part, and therefore there is very little about Baal worship and idolatry in this book. No, Isaiah is concerned with a city's life, with the structure of a community. It is in the life of this city, says the prophet, that the divine torah or teaching is being violated (1:21-23). The city's commerce and government and law courts have done violence to the will of God. And so the judgment from God will destroy the foundations of the city's life—her government and officials, her military and clergy, her wheelers and dealers and movers (3:1-15). "O my people, your leaders mislead you, and confuse the course of your paths," says the prophet (3:12).

It follows therefore that salvation will not have come, in Isaiah's view, until the city will again have become faithful, until the government is righteous and just (9:7; 11:4-5) and counselors and judges are wise and upright (1:26). Indeed, the kingdom of God will have come, proclaims Isaiah, when all nations go up to such a city to learn God's ways from tradition and torah and to walk obediently according to his teachings. Then and only then will all governments beat their swords into plow-shares and their spears into pruning hooks; "nation shall not lift up sword against nation, neither shall they learn war any more" (2:1-4). The city of God—the city that has foundations, whose builder and maker is God—that is really the vision the prophet Isaiah holds out before our eyes, and, of course, no prophecy could be more pertinent to our maddened world.

## Literary Contents

As many of you know, the book divides itself very easily into sections. Chapters 1—12 are oracles against Judah and Jerusalem, ending with a doxology in chapter 12. Chapters 13—23 are made up of oracles, some of them non-Isaianic (chaps. 13—14, maybe 23), against various foreign enemies of Israel; but after the pattern of Amos, the section climaxes with a specific prophecy against Judah and, in fact, against two of her officials (22:1-14, 15-25). Chapters 24—27 have often been called apocalyptic and assigned a postexilic date, and while the section probably does not come from Isaiah and has apocalyptic elements in it, it is not a unity, consisting variously of apocalyptic judgments, salvation oracles, laments, and judgment oracles. Surprisingly, however, it is from this section that the lectionary often draws. With chapter 28, the genuine oracles of judgment against Judah are taken up again and run through chapter 33. Chapters 34—35 have often been attributed to Second Isaiah, and perhaps the most we can say is that they are from the Isaiah school. Chapters 36—39 form a historical appendix largely paralleling portions of 2 Kings 18:3, 17—20:19, with some omissions and additions. With chapter 40, Second Isaiah begins.

The book has obvious indications of having been edited. There are superscriptions at the beginning of chapters 1, 2, and 13. Chapter 12 seems to form a liturgical conclusion to the first section. Chapters 5 and 9, which carry the same refrain (5:25; 9:12, 17, 21) have been separated from each other by the prose sections of chapters 6—8. Chapters 7 and 20 both describe the actions of Isaiah in the third person. It seems very likely therefore that the book, which first circulated in the form of smaller collections, has been assembled by the disciples of Isaiah (cf. 8:16) and that they are responsible for the third-person sections. It also seems very likely that the disciples of Isaiah of Jerusalem formed an ongoing school, which attached Second and Third Isaiah to the book, and, indeed, out of which school the authors of Second and Third Isaiah came. It is my personal view, set forth in my commentary on Third Isaiah (*The Community and Message of Isaiah 56—66* [Minneapolis: Augsburg Pub. House, 1982]), that this Isaiah school joined forces with the deuteronomic, levitical reform school that was responsible for the Book of Deuteronomy some time before 538 B.C.E., and that the joining then gave rise to the compilation of Third Isaiah. But that is not the subject of this essay. At any rate, I think the Isaiah school was responsible for the Book of Isaiah as we now have it, and we all are deeply indebted to their faithfulness and legacy.

The book must be read against its historical background, and despite Brevard Childs's more sweeping canonical views, I really do not think any portion of the Isaiah corpus can be understood apart from its historical background. Chapters 1—8 have to be understood in the context of the Syro-Ephraimitic crisis of 735-733 B.C.E., which threatened the Davidic throne in Judah. And the whole has to be seen in the light of Assyria's resurgence and its three invasions into the west and Palestine, under Tiglath-pileser III, Sargon II, and Sennacherib. We are dealing with the motif of power in the Book of Isaiah, with the power of a nation's leaders and of the Davidic throne, with the power of a revived Assyrian empire, but most of all we are dealing with the power of God. And it is with the conflicts among these powers and with the proper relation to such powers that our prophet is primarily concerned. Certainly in an age such as ours, where political, military, and economic powers seem to rule the day, that topic can command our attention.

Who really holds all power in his hands, according to the prophet Isaiah? The answer of course is God, but the way in which Isaiah sets that forth for us is marvelous to behold.

## Major Themes of Isaiah

### The Holy One of Israel

First of all, there is the call of Isaiah, in chapter 6, and the witness to the person of God in that call really strikes the principal notes that will sound forth through all of the rest of the prophet's oracles. The rest of this essay will show how that is so.

King Uzziah died in 742 B.C.E.—Uzziah, that great king, who reigned forty-one years in Judah (783–742); who repaired the defenses of Jerusalem, and reorganized and refitted the army; who imposed his rule over Edomite lands and secured the north-south trade routes; who thrust his frontier deep into Philistine territory and into the southern desert; who had farmers and vinedressers in the hills and in the fertile lands, "for he loved the soil," says Chronicles; who dug cisterns in the arid wilderness; and who invented new siege defenses for Jerusalem. When that great king, "who became very strong," says the Chronicler (2 Chron. 26:1–21), died, punished by his Lord with leprosy for his proud power, Isaiah was confronted with the real King. "I saw the Lord, sitting upon a throne, high and lifted up"—enthroned there in his heavenly temple, surrounded by his seraphic messengers, with just the train of his royal robe sufficient to fill the temple of heaven, with the foundations of the universe shaking at his royal presence, and the whole place filled up with the smoke from the fiery glory of the Lord.

Isaiah meets the real King, the real power in the person of his Lord, and he hears that this power is other than all human and earthly power. The empires of earth exercise their own petty power, but it is nothing compared to God's. "The Egyptians are men, and not God; and their horses are flesh, and not spirit" (31:3). The power of God is the power of the Holy One. "Holy, holy, holy is the Lord of hosts," sing the seraphim in that antiphonal song in Isaiah's call. To say that God is holy is to say that he is totally other than anything in all creation. As the second commandment of the Decalogue puts it, other than anything that is in the heavens above or that is on the earth beneath, or that is in the waters under the earth—totally unique, totally different, totally other Creator God from all that he has created.

There is something perverse about our theology these days. We somehow want to confuse the Creator with the things he has created. We want to bind up and capture him in the structures and processes of this world. And so we say with J. A. T. Robinson or Paul Tillich that he is the Ground of all Being. Or we join the nature worshipers in our congregations and identify God with some great soul of nature, and then we find him revealed in the beauty of lakes and trees. Or we become process theologians and make God the power of natural and human evolving. Or we turn him into a birthing goddess, from whose being all things and persons have come forth, and then we find him incarnate in everything and even in ourselves, until we say with Virginia Mollenkott that "our milieu is divine" (*The Divine Feminine* [New York: Crossroad, 1983], 109), or with Carol Christ, "I found God in myself and I loved her fiercely" (*Womenspirit Rising* [San Francisco: Harper & Row, 1979], 277).

But not according to this prophet Isaiah—not according to Isaiah! This God of the Bible is holy God, other than all in this world. And so we are not to worship the creation in the place of its Creator, as St. Paul also pointed out (Rom. 1:25). As in Isa. 8:12-13, "Do not fear what [this people] fear, nor be in dread. But the Lord of hosts, him you shall regard as holy; let him be your fear, and let him be your dread." And if we reject that, we become like those rebellious people in Isa. 30:8-11, "who will not hear the instruction of the Lord; who say to the seers, 'See not'; and to the prophets, 'Prophesy not to us what is right; speak to us smooth things, prophesy illusions, leave the way, turn aside from the path, let us hear no more of the Holy One of Israel.'"

We must not overlook the fact, however, that this Holy One is "of Israel." Only three times in the Old Testament is God called just the Holy One, without the prepositional phrase "of Israel" attached (Isa. 40:25; Hos. 11:9; Hab. 3:3). This God of total otherness from us, this

God of "terrifying power," as Isa. 10:33 puts it, is ultimate power who wills to enter into covenant relationship with a people—with the Israel of the Old Testament and with the new Israel, the church, of the New. This absolutely transcendent Lord enters into fellowship with the work of his hands (Isa. 29:23), with a people whom he has expressly created for himself. We are joined in a covenant bond with the Power that made and runs the universe.

So it is important for us to know further the nature of such Power, and Isaiah tells us in his report of his call that God is also moral Power—unblemished purity, of righteousness and justice. As Isa. 5:16 phrases it, " . . . the Lord of hosts is exalted in justice, and the Holy God shows himself holy in righteousness." He differs from us—is totally other from us—in that he is absolutely righteous, perfectly fulfilling his relationship with his creation and his covenant people. And over against that purity, revealed to his eyes, the prophet cries out, "Woe to me, for I am lost, for I am a man of unclean lips, and I dwell in the midst of a people of unclean lips; for the King mine eyes have seen, the Lord of hosts" (Isa. 6:5).

## Israel's Pride

Our sin is revealed when our natures are contrasted with God's—for us Christians, when we see the glory of God shining in the face of Jesus Christ and stand at the foot of his cross; for the prophets, when they rehearse the enduring love and faithfulness of God toward Israel and contrast it with Israel's rebellion. "Sons and daughters have I reared and brought up," laments God the Father in Isaiah 1, "But they have rebelled against me. The ox knows its owner, and the ass its master's crib [cf. Luke's Christmas story], but Israel does not know, my people does not understand."

What care the Father has poured into rearing and bringing up those children! Isaiah puts it in the terms of his famous song of the vineyard (chap. 5). Israel was the vine and the Lord, the beloved, the vinedresser. He planted the vine on a very fertile hill. He dug in the soil and cleared it of stones, and planted the very finest vines. He built a watchtower in the midst of the field, and hewed out a vat from a rock to store the wine. And "what more was there to do for my vineyard that I have not done in it?" God asks. Yet, the vine has brought forth *bᵉ'ušîm*—grapes that stink and are good for nothing. And Isaiah acknowledges his common guilt with such an ungrateful people—I am of unclean lips as are all my compatriots. "None is righteous; no not one," and so none can stand before their moral God. For the righteous God cannot dwell with unrighteous human beings, and if we approach him in our unclean, corrupted condition, we shall be burned up by the fire of his moral purity—in Isaiah's metaphor, "The light of Israel will become a fire, and his Holy One a flame; and it will burn and devour [our] thorns and briers in one day" (10:17). Woe to me, woe to us, for we are lost, proclaims Isaiah.

The prophet is very specific about our sin, since we are Israel—the "Israel of God," Paul calls the church (Gal. 6:16). To be sure, Isaiah acknowledges that we are a very religious people. His description of us in 1:12 could apply to any of our Easter or Christmas services: "When you come to appear before me, who requires of you this trampling of my courts?"—that vast throng of supposed worshipers, crowding into God's sanctuary. It should come as a shock to us that God hates our worship—we often think we are doing him a favor when we go to church. But God tells us, in the words of Isaiah, "Bring no more vain offerings . . . I cannot endure iniquity and solemn assembly" (Isa. 1:13). God cannot endure the church services of an iniquitous people. Indeed, far from adhering to our sentimental belief that he hears every prayer, the Lord tells us in this passage, "When you spread forth your hands, I will hide my eyes from you; even though you make many prayers, I will not listen." For, says the Lord, those hands you raise to me in prayer are hands dyed with blood—for Isaiah, and certainly also for us, the blood of the dying poor denied their right in society and in the law courts; the blood of parishioners denied God's good life by faithless preacher and phony priest; the blood of those lied to by government officials and prompted to put their trust in military might; the blood of those ignored, forgotten, oppressed by the complacent makers of false promises and covenants.

I sometimes believe we have only to think of the children of our time to sense the depth of Isaiah's indictment against us—children on the one hand abused, or on the other totally undisciplined; children turned over to the television set for hours on end; children given AIDS by their drug-addicted mothers; or children bounced back and forth like ping-pong balls between homes and schools by their divorced parents. Yes, our hands and those of our society are covered with the blood of our children, one-quarter of them the victims of abortion before they are even born, the placentas and the fetal material used then to make cosmetics to beautify those complacent women Isaiah describes so well in chapter 3.

We sinners have, says Isaiah in 28:14-15, made a covenant with death. That is, we have agreed to sacrifice to and worship death in order to save our own lives, like Faust selling his soul to the devil in exchange for his own pleasure and security. And we well might ask how that language of Isaiah's applies to our time. What have we been willing to sacrifice to death for the sake of preserving ourselves and our comforts—the lives of our children, but also the lives of North American Indians in exchange for land and oil and gold? The blood, sweat, and tears of Chinese laborers for the completion of a transcontinental railroad? The lives of thousands of Vietnamese for national pride and phony honor? Isaiah's message illumines so well the nature of our sinfulness.

But what is the primary sin, according to the book of this prophet? It is the sin of pride—the pride that makes us wise in our own eyes and shrewd in our own sight (5:21); the pride that causes us to reject the law of the Lord and to despise his Word (5:24) in the belief that they are just silly precepts for children or are for someone else (28:9-10); the pride that believes we can save our own lives by the exercise of our earthly power (30:15-16); the pride that believes we can manipulate God by empty ritual, while reserving our hearts and loves for our selfish selves (29:14). We look at all our accomplishments, and we boast with the King of Assyria: "By the strength of my hand I have done it, and by my wisdom, for I have understanding" (10:22). And we do indeed turn ourselves into our own gods and goddesses, as did also ancient Babylon. "I will ascend to heaven," declares that society in its heart (Isa. 14:14). "Above the stars of God I will set my throne on high . . . I will ascend above the heights of the clouds, I will make myself like the Most High."

That has always been our sin, according to the Old Testament. "Come, let us build ourselves a city, and a tower with its top in the heavens, and let us make a name for ourselves," we said at the Tower of Babel (Gen. 11:4). "Come, you can be like God, knowing good and evil," the serpent told us in the garden of Eden (Gen. 3:4-5). And so, woe to me, woe to us, cries Isaiah, for we are lost; for the King our eyes have seen, the Lord of hosts.

The result is, in the Book of Isaiah, that God's judgments are leveled largely against our pride and Judah's—against the highhanded rebellion that makes us think that we can run our own lives and be our own gods and goddesses in the world. And those judgments, according to Isaiah, are valid for both contemporary and future audiences.

In that marvelous passage in chapter 28, a woe oracle directed to the proud "drunkards of Ephraim and to the fading flower of its glorious beauty, which is on the head of the rich valley" (v.1), Isaiah challenges those proud leaders and clergy who have been making fun of his prophecy. "Whom will he teach knowledge, and to whom will he explain the message?" the scoffers ask. "Children? For it is precept upon precept, line upon line, here a little, there a little"—the Word of the Lord is for these skeptics like a nursery rhyme taught to children. And so Isaiah takes up the words of that taunt and turns them into an oracle of judgment. And he says that Judah will not only be destroyed by the overwhelming flood of the Assyrian army, but the judgment on Judah will indeed be line upon line, here a little, there a little. For its proud leaders will also be the immediate victims of the slow, inexorable ticktock of God's judgments in the movement of time. Here a little, there a little, the Word of God destroying our life—bringing the gradual growth of fate, the monotonous stages of decay: ambition turned to empty envy, pride soured by loneliness and hatred, selfishness searching desperately for some new thing to feed its ego. God judges us in all the little things of life, says the prophet—in the terrible simplicity of everyday. Line upon line, here a little, there a little: in the dissatisfactions that rob our peace, and the troubles that disrupt our families; in the fears that come with a dark street at night, and the anxieties about our work on the morrow. Here a little, there a little, God's judgments work their way, until, in the words of the prophet, we "go, and fall backward and are broken and snared and taken" (Isa. 28:13). That is one form of the judgment against pride in Isaiah's book.

## The Divine Plan

But then of course there is the judgment against Judah's rebellion in the form of the Assyrian armies, who will shortly deport the ten northern tribes, to be lost forever from history, and who will ravage Judah and Benjamin in the time of Hezekiah. This God of Isaiah's, this Holy One of Israel, is the Lord over all the nations. He can just whistle for Assyria to attack his people (5:27; 7:26), and that empire can be used by him as the rod of the divine wrath (10:5). Or in 17:13, this Holy God can rebuke the attackers and send them fleeing away, like dust before the wind. It is this coming judgment, using Assyria, which is revealed to the prophet at the time of his call.

Preachers sometimes employ Isaiah's call narrative (chap. 6) as a model of Christian discipleship. When the prophet hears the divine question, "Whom shall I send, and who will go for us?" and replies with the words, "Here am I! Send me" (6:8), we often think that is a marvelous response of dedication and service, and we urge our congregations also to reply, "Here am I, send me." But we stop there and never go on to tell the awful mission on which Isaiah is sent. He is to "make the heart of this people fat, and their ears heavy, and shut their eyes" (6:10)—that is, Isaiah's preaching is intended to make the people even more stubborn and rebellious, so that God's judgment, using Assyria against them, will be even more deserved. Isaiah, hearing that awful commission, cries out, "How long, O Lord?" And the Lord replies, "Until cities lie waste without inhabitant, and houses without people, and the land is utterly desolate, and the Lord removes the people far away, and the forsaken places are many in the midst of the land" (6:11).

One of the major motifs in the Book of Isaiah is that God has a plan—a design he is working out in history. Part of that plan is the destruction of Judah's pride, so that Isaiah's preaching, which makes the people even more rebellious, is simply an instrument of the plan. Isaiah is given to know the plan, just as Paul says in 1 Corinthians 2 that he knows the secret and hidden wisdom of God, decreed before the ages and revealed through the Spirit of Christ (vv. 6–16). Isaiah knows the plan—it is revealed to him by God; as in 28:26, he is instructed aright, and his God teaches him. To disregard this plan, to rely on one's own wisdom, and to reject the Word of God are utter folly: "Woe to those who are wise in their own eyes, and shrewd in their own sight" (5:21). Thus we read in 29:13–14: "Because this people draw near with their mouth and honor me with their lips, while their hearts are far from me, and their fear of me is a commandment of men learned by rote; therefore, behold, I will again do marvelous things with this people, wonderful and marvelous—that is, in judgment—and the wisdom of their wise men shall perish, and the discernment of their discerning men shall be hid." God's plan will put to shame all our wise schemes for our own futures.

Even though Assyria is an instrument of the plan of this Holy One of

Israel, nevertheless if Assyria oversteps its bounds as a mere instrument of God, it too will be destroyed. "Shall the axe vaunt itself over him who hews with it, or the saw magnify itself against him who wields it?" (10:15). No. "As I have planned, so shall it be," says the Lord in 14:24–27, "and as I have purposed, so shall it stand, that I will break the Assyrian in my land. . . . For the Lord of hosts has purposed, and who will annul it? His hand is stretched out, and who will turn it back?"

The final part of God's plan, then, is that he be acknowledged as Lord in all the earth—that the whole earth be full of his glory, of esteem and honor for him (6:3)—that the earth be full of the knowledge of his lordship as the waters cover the sea (11:9). When that day comes, then the serpent of our evil rebellion against our God will be turned into harmlessness. "The sucking child shall play over the hole of the asp, and the weaned child shall put his hand on the adder's den. They shall not hurt or destroy in all my holy mountain" (11:8–9).

Ultimately, the judgment of God consists in doing away with our sinful pride, which has caused us to try to be our own gods and goddesses. This is set forth in eschatological terms in Isaiah's magnificent portrayal of the Day of the Lord, in 2:6–22. We have bowed down to the work of our hands, says the prophet, and to what our own fingers have made, and so we must be humbled and brought low, and it is the majesty of the glory of the Lord himself that will be revealed. Then every proud and lofty creation of humankind, which has so fostered our pride—everything that is proud and lofty, all that is lifted up and high—will be shown to be as nothing before the Holy One of Israel. "Enter into the rock, and hide in the dust," proclaims the prophet in the refrain that divides this passage, "from before the terror of the Lord, and from the glory of his majesty. For the haughty looks of humankind shall be brought low, and the pride of peoples shall be humbled; and the Lord alone will be exalted in that day" (Isa. 2:10–11). Isaiah is saying that if we want peace on earth and the coming of the kingdom of God, then we also must want the total humbling by our God of our rebellious pride.

### Forgiveness and Trust:
### The Stance of Obedience

We have skipped a portion of the call of Isaiah 6, of course, in this explication of its themes, and that is the part in verses 6 and 7 in which the prophet is forgiven. The Holy One of Israel is not only ultimate, other Power; he is not only the Lord of all nations and the Judge of all the earth; but he is also that one who alone has the power to overcome our sin. And so, in the call narrative, a seraphic messenger cleanses the prophet's lips with a coal from the altar and tells him, "Your guilt is taken away, and your sin is forgiven." God's alone is the power that can forgive us our sins (cf. Mark 2:1-12).

The prophet holds out to his rebellious countrymen and women the invitation to forgiveness. In 1:18-20: "Come now, let us reason together . . . though your sins are like scarlet, they shall be as white as snow; though they are red like crimson, they shall become like wool. If you are willing and obedient, you shall eat the good of the land; But if you refuse and rebel, you shall be devoured by the sword, for the mouth of the Lord has spoken."

That brings us finally to ask, What is the primary requirement God has for his people in the covenant relationship, according to the prophecies of Isaiah? What is it that we are to do, in relationship to our Lord? Certainly Isaiah has a great deal to say about ethical and just dealings within the community, as we have seen. And certainly he says a great deal about sincere worship and obedience to the commands and teachings of God, as we have noted. But at the root of these, as their basis and context, is our total stance before this Holy One of Israel. Our proper response to such a God, says Isaiah, is a life of trust—trust in which we give up our reliance on our own defense, our own wisdom, our own security and plans for the future, and place our lives in God's hands, to be guided according to his wise plan and secured and made whole by his power.

Indeed, says Isaiah, the new Jerusalem in the kingdom of God will have as its founding fathers and mothers such persons of trust. "For behold, I am laying in Zion for a foundation . . . a precious cornerstone, of a sure foundation." And written on that cornerstone are the words "He who believes will not be in haste" (Isa. 28:16). That is, persons who believe and trust God will not search about frantically for ways to save their own lives, but they will in quiet and confidence grasp the hand of their all-powerful and merciful God. Such persons of faith will, says Isaiah, form the cornerstone of the city of God.

Isaiah pictures trust primarily, however, in his dealings with the kings of Judah. Thus, during the reign of Hezekiah (715–687/6 B.C.E.), when that king and his officials want to break free of the Assyrian yoke by military alliance with Egypt, Isaiah tells them, according to chapter 30, that by all their efforts to save their lives they will lose them instead, because they are not acting according to God's plan and counsel. "Woe to the rebellious children," says the Lord, "who carry out a plan, but not mine; . . . who set out to go down to Egypt without asking for my counsel, to take refuge in the protection of Pharaoh, and to seek shelter in the shadow of Egypt!" (vv. 1–2). And then in verse 15, "For thus says the Lord God, the Holy One of Israel, 'In returning and rest you shall be saved; in quietness and in trust shall be your strength.' And you would not, but you said, 'No! We will speed upon horses'" (16a). "Therefore," the judgment of the Lord is "You shall speed away" (16b), that is, into captivity. Because God holds the world in his hand, only trust in him can save our lives.

But of course the most famous passage is that one in Isaiah 7 in which the prophet begs King Ahaz to place his trust in God's promise to the house of David. It is the time of the Syro-Ephraimitic alliance, in 735 B.C.E. The giant of the resurgent Assyrian empire has once more set its greedy eyes on the west. A century earlier a coalition of minor states had turned back a similar Assyrian threat, and Syria and Ephraim want to form the same coalition again. But Ahaz of Judah, a fearful soul, wants nothing to do with the scheme. So Ephraim and Syria threaten to attack Judah and to put one favorable to their cause on Judah's throne.

In that dangerous situation, the Lord commands Isaiah, "Go forth to meet Ahaz, you and Shearjashub, your son, at the end of the conduit of the upper pool on the highway to the Fuller's Field" (Isa. 7:3). What a marvelous God this is; he is so concerned about our lives that he gives his prophet specific highway directions! Ahaz is out there examining Jerusalem's water supply, in case of siege. And the message that Isaiah is to take to Ahaz is "be quiet, do not fear, and do not let your heart be faint, because of these two smoldering stumps of firebrands, Ephraim and Syria" (Isa. 7:4). These are only men, after all, while God is the Lord of nations, with a plan, and he has made a promise to the house of David that its throne shall never fall. But trust is the condition—trust in the power and working of this promising God. And so, says the Lord through his prophet, "If you will not believe, you shall not be established" (Isa. 7:9).

On the face of it, it must have seemed like a ridiculous promise to Ahaz—that God was offering him a little babe to bolster his belief. Ahaz did not need a baby then; Ahaz needed an army! And because he would not believe, he was not established.

In fact, to prompt Ahaz's trust, God offers to give him a sign: a young woman—possibly the wife of the king or the wife of the prophet himself—"shall conceive and bear a son and call his name Immanuel" (Isa. 7:14), and before the child is even two years old, the threat of Syria and Ephraim will disappear. If Ahaz will trust that promise and trust that sign, if he will believe, he surely will be established.

We too think we need armies and goods, advanced degrees and status and power, material comforts and self-fulfillment and all sorts of things to save our lives in this world. But as with Ahaz of old, God gives us for our assurance only a helpless babe. We celebrate his birth in Bethlehem every Christmas season. And really, the message is still the same as it was back there in the time of Isaiah—that if we will trust that sign and the power and the purity, the plan and the mercy of the God who sent him, then our lives will be saved, not only now, but for all eternity. If we do believe—if we trust the Holy One of Israel—then surely, yes, surely indeed, we shall be established.

# 2

# Isaiah's Royal Theology and the Messiah

James Luther Mays

## Isaiah: Prophet of the Messiah?

I am going to use a psalm as a way of talking about the context of Isaiah's theology. There are reasons. First, the theology assumed in the prophecy of Isaiah is to be found in express form in the psalms. Second, I want to focus on the trajectory of messianic theology in the Bible, and to do that, I need to begin in psalmic territory.

The way the Old Testament is often taught and studied makes a special problem for Isaiah. If you follow the order of the Hebrew Bible, and work your way through the Torah, and then the former prophets, that's fine for Jeremiah. To read Jeremiah, one needs to know Deuteronomy, and in that approach, one has dealt with Deuteronomy. And that's fine for Ezekiel. To read Ezekiel, one needs to know the material in the Torah that is usually called the priestly document, and one has dealt with that. But to read Isaiah, one needs to know the Psalms, and they are over there waiting to be dealt with later in such a sequence.

Isaiah's thought and speech about God are controlled by a vision that has three features. First, Adonai is a royal deity, a sovereign, exalted above earth, exalted above the nation. Second, Adonai has chosen Jerusalem as his city and called it Zion. It is the earthly seat of his reign, and the sphere in which his policy is to be observed. Third, as his human agent to represent his rule, Adonai has chosen the Davidic king and installed him as the anointed one. Simply put, Adonai is sovereign; there

39

is a city of God; and there is a son of God. Isaiah understands God and God's way with his people and the nations in terms of that primary vision. The home of this vision, the place where in the canon of the Old Testament that vision is *sui generis*, is the so-called enthronement psalms (47, 93, 95—100), and two other related groups of psalms, the Songs of Zion (e.g. 46, 48, 76) and the royal psalms—here I would emphasize 2, 110, and certainly 132.

It is certainly easy to imagine that when Isaiah saw Adonai sitting upon a throne, high and lifted up, connected to earth through the train of his garments down to the Jerusalem temple, he had been listening to, or perhaps even participating in, the chant of Psalm 99. "The Lord reigns," says that psalm. "He sits enthroned upon the cherubim. Let the earth quake" (v. 1). And you remember Isaiah 6: the thresholds did quake under the very feet of Isaiah. The psalm has three stanzas, each concluded by the refrain "Holy is he" (vv. 3, 5, 9), a repetition echoed in the chant of the seraphim in Isaiah's vision, "Holy, holy, holy is the Lord of hosts."

When Isaiah refers to the people of God, he names them Jerusalem or Zion. He thinks of the people of God as the subjects of the heavenly king whose dwelling place is in Zion. "God is in the midst of her; she shall not be moved" (Ps. 46:5). Zion is for Isaiah the reliable city (Isa. 1:26). The city is a trustworthy refuge, because within her citadels God has shown himself a sure defense (Psalms 46, 48). When Isaiah speaks of the one whose name will be called "Wonderful, Counselor, Mighty God, Everlasting Father, Prince of Peace" (Isa. 9:6), he is formulating a conception of the identity and role of the Davidic king that is spelled out in the royal psalms. When Isaiah dealt with the kings of Judah, he took their office as the chosen regent of the Lord far more seriously than they did. Remember, for instance, chapter 7: Ahaz was terrified during the Syro-Ephraimite crisis because his neighbors to the north had conspired to overthrow him and put him off the throne, and put another, more cooperative person on the throne. Isaiah told Ahaz, "If you will not believe, surely you will not be established" (v. 9). Believe what? The text does not say, but you, the reader, are supposed to know that Ahaz was installed in rituals represented by the royal psalms. God had put him in place; no human power could displace him (Ps. 2:6). So, if you want to understand Isaiah better, go read the Psalms. Incidentally, that applies not only to First Isaiah, but also to what we call Second and Third Isaiah.

Such then is the general apology for talking about Isaiah by means of a psalm. But the particular reason is this: I want to say a word in favor of reading Isaiah as the prophet of the messiah. The traditional Christian view of Isaiah up to the rise of modern criticism was that he was the messianic prophet above all others. The Book of Isaiah is used in the New Testament more than any of the other prophetic books. In the lections from the Old Testament used in most lectionaries today, Isaiah is still read that way. The emphasis is on chapters 6, 7, 9, and 11, the passages about Emmanuel and the child and the shoot from the stump of Jesse; and the season is predominantly Advent, Christmas, and Epiphany. Historical criticism has called this view of Isaiah into question. It says that the two explicit messianic passages in chapters 9 and 11 are in no sense predictions of a Christ to come centuries in the future, as the church had always believed. And some scholars, as you know, have concluded that these sayings do not belong to Isaiah of Jerusalem in any case, but are to be dated down in a late eschatologically oriented, postexilic period.

What is needed is to move off the narrow base of these two explicit messianic oracles and the question of their relationship to the New Testament to an understanding of the broader royal theology with which Isaiah thinks and speaks, an understanding which recognizes that it is messianic in character per se. We need to view Isaiah in the context of a trajectory of messianic thought concerned with the role in the reign of God of the figure who is called king, seed of David, servant of God, messiah, son of God.

## Psalm 2 and Isaiah

One way to illustrate that approach is to take one of the psalms that lie behind Isaiah's theology, explore its intellectual world, and then trace its connection with Isaiah and the New Testament. I have chosen Psalm 2 because of the structural relation of its themes to Isaiah's prophecy, and because of its use in the New Testament to identify Jesus in the Gospels (e.g., Mark 1:11 and parallels).

Why do the nations conspire,
 and the peoples plot in vain?
The kings of the earth set themselves,
 and the rulers take counsel together,
  against the Lord and his anointed, saying,

"Let us burst their bonds asunder, and cast their cords from us."
He who sits in the heavens laughs;
   the Lord has them in derision,
Then he will speak to them in his wrath,
   and terrify them in his fury, saying,
"I have set my king
   on Zion, my holy hill."
I will tell of the decree of the Lord:
He said to me, "You are my son,
   today I have begotten you.
Ask of me, and I will make the nations your heritage,
   and the ends of the earth your possession.
You shall break them with a rod of iron,
   and dash them in pieces like a potter's vessel."
Now therefore, O kings, be wise;
   be warned, O rulers of the earth.
Serve the Lord with fear,
   with trembling kiss his feet,
lest he be angry, and you perish in the way;
   for his wrath is quickly kindled.
Blessed are all who take refuge in him.

In the light of what has already been said, the fabric of connections between Psalm 2 and Isaiah's prophecy should be apparent. In Psalm 2 the Lord is a sovereign monarch enthroned in the heavens. Zion is the mount made holy by God's selection of it as his. There the Lord has set a human being who is God's king, messiah, son. The conspiring and plotting of the nations is viewed as a rebellion against God and God's messiah—precisely the view Isaiah took, you remember, of the alliance between Syria and Ephraim (Isa. 7:1-9; 8:11-15). The Lord uses a human instrument as the rod of his anger against the arrogance of nations and their rulers. In the Psalms it is the messiah; in Isaiah, of course, it is Assyria (10:5). When Isaiah says, "Unto us a child is born, unto us a son is given," he does not mean that somebody has just had a baby (9:6). He means that what happens in this psalm, the inauguration of a king, has just happened or is going to happen in Judah. The fabric of connections between psalm and prophecy is almost complete.

There is no question, I think, about the subject of this remarkable poem. If we apply the principle of repetition, the answer is obvious. The nations and their kings appear in every one of the four stanzas. The psalm is consummately concerned with the world of politics and history, the peoples and their governments. The purpose of the psalm is clear in the progress of thought through the parts. It sets forth the relation between the kingdom of heaven and the kingdoms of earth, a relationship at whose focus stands the figure called messiah and son. Through that figure, whose royalty is the creation of the divine reign, God, says the psalm, is dealing with the powers of this earth. But it is just the clarity of theme and purpose that sharpens the central question about the psalm: Who is the one named king, messiah, son of God? The psalm does not say, and we must not think too quickly with the New Testament here. We know the answer, but we do not know what the answer means, unless we understand the role of this psalm as the origin of the messianic trajectory and the way that trajectory passes through and is transformed by prophets like Isaiah. When Jesus is called son of God, it means he enters into a role that is prepared both by the general experience of humanity and the prophetic insight that belongs to Isaiah. Only from texts like Psalm 2 and their relation to prophecy can we know into what office he enters and what expectation he fulfills in that, according to the Gospels, he appears as king, messiah, son of God.

## Royal Psalms in Judah and the Ancient Near East

In its Old Testament context, to what does the title "son of God" point? Recognizing the genre or type of Psalm 2 provides the first partial answer. It belongs to a group of ten or more psalms which are usually classified in Old Testament textbooks as royal psalms. The basic characteristic holding them together is that they all have, as their central subject, a living, reigning king of Judah. In occasion and function, these psalms are quite varied. The group includes corporate petitions for the king, prayers by him and for him before and after battle, a song for a royal wedding, pieces particularly belonging to the ritual of his accession to office. In all this variety, these psalms serve one purpose: they speak of the place that the office of the king has in the faith of Israel. They witness that the king has a focal role in Israel's status, welfare, and destiny under God. In this function, Psalm 2 and the rest of the royal psalms are part of a wider literature of a similar kind. Such prayers, songs, rituals appear in the known literature of the nations of the ancient

Near East from the Nile to the Mesopotamian areas. Royal psalms have a context that is broader than Israel and its specific faith, and the implication is clear: only by reading them within this broader context will they be fully understood. And in particular, only in this way can we learn the full import of the question, To whom does the title "son of God" refer? What does it mean that it is used for a quite human, political, mortal figure?

First, and perhaps least important, we can understand in this way why certain language is used in this psalm and in the Psalms and prophets generally—language which seems harsh and bizarre. Take verse 9, for instance. Part of the promise to the son that he will possess the nations of the earth says, "You will break them with a rod of iron and dash them in pieces like a potter's vessel." Read literally, those two lines seem cruel and pointless. They smack of an insane tyranny that possesses only to destroy. But in its original sphere of use, these words were not meant that way at all. Behind them is a ritual known particularly from the ceremonies of Egypt as part of the procedures of installing a king. The names of all the nations over which Pharaoh claimed sovereignty would be written on clay tablets, and in a symbolic ritual, the king would smash those tablets with his scepter. Translated, his dramatic ritual language simply means, You shall claim them and rule them; they belong to your hegemony. These illuminations of the language of the text show us that in these psalms Israel has taken up and entered into a sphere of expression that was common to the social history of its world and age. It was language prepared by general human history to speak about what Israel and its inspiration wanted and had to speak about—the question of power on earth and its relation to God.

Second, by comparing the psalm with the royal traditions of other peoples, we can be more certain of what is happening in the psalm, of the transaction that its language represents. Analogies with the literature of Mesopotamia and especially Egypt make it clear that the psalm belongs to one moment in the ritual of the inauguration of a monarch. The accession usually consisted of two main acts. The king was crowned in the sanctuary, where he received the royal record containing the actual commission to rule given by the deity, and usually in addition the king's new throne name. After he had been crowned, he was then conducted to his palace, where he ascended the throne and in a more or less threatening way announced in a general proclamation the start of his rule—a sort of inaugural address. Psalm 2 most certainly has its place here. The king who reads the psalm is reporting the commission to rule that had been given him in the sanctuary and is stating his international policy. Now the significance of the somewhat mysterious question that opens the psalm in verses 1 and 2 comes into view. At the time of the change of rulers, all the vassals would use the shift as an opportunity to rebel. The accession of a new king would then by custom and ritual be an occasion for asserting the authority of the king's office anew, for construing any moves toward independence as rebellion.

Incidentally, when you think about Judah's situation, about the actuality of the political situation in which Psalm 2 was used, then the incredible boldness of the procedure is astonishing. Judah was a county-sized kingdom, and Jerusalem was a kind of county-seat capital, a little town. The language of Psalm 2 might have sounded a bit more credible in the capitals of the great empires of the ancient world, in Thebes and in Babylon and in Ashur. But in Jerusalem? Viewed in the cold eye of historical reality, it rises to the heights of ridiculousness. But behind this boldness is a confidence that Adonai alone is God, and that the king whom he selects is the one of whom all this language used in the ancient world can alone be truthfully said. And it was said, against all appearances, in unbearable tension with reality, over and over again in Judah.

Third, in the context of the thought world of other peoples, we can see the crucial importance for human existence of the event in which one is named son of God. The designation of a king had its background in an ancient process as old as the social order itself. This process was at work wherever and whenever, in the deep history of the ancient Near East, a group of human beings felt compelled to recognize one above the others, was led by the need to deal with the question of power and the quest for power within their social group and in competition with others. The leader became the agent of power and the source of power. In the societies of the ancient Near East known to us, it was believed that power flowed from the deity to the people through the king. He, the king, was the provision for three basic needs of society: for security against enemies, he was the leader in warfare; for justice and order, he was the judge par excellence; for well-being, the integrity of his relation to the gods was the channel of blessing.

That such a view of the king was held in Judah is evident from another of the royal psalms, Psalm 72, where the congregation itemizes precisely these three expectations of the king in a prayer in his behalf. "May he judge the people with righteousness," says the prayer, "and the poor with justice. Let the mountains bear prosperity for the people and the hills in righteousness. . . . May his foes bow down before him, and his enemies lick the dust" (vv. 2–3, 9).

We may notice here that some things never change. In our modern times it would be unthinkable for somebody to run for the presidency of the United States without having a platform dealing with national defense, law and order, and prosperity. These have been the three foundations of power in human society from the earliest time that we have any records.

Now when the king was named son of God, the title was a confession of faith that the king was the representative and agent of the deity in such unity and coherence that only the term "son" could display the correspondence and claims between the two. How that reality to which the title pointed was created was conceived of in a variety of ways in the general culture. But common to all of them was the belief that the king was a divine instrument of life for those whom he ruled. So when the psalm was recited by a Davidide in Jerusalem, it was a proclamation that the Lord had chosen to provide life through the office in which he was installed; the inauguration of his reign created the opportunity for blessing or for perishing. Depending on the response to the announcement of his kingship, he was there as a chance for the world to live in the reign of God, to find refuge and not perish.

The second psalm gathers all this background of social and religious experience into Israel's theology. It can address itself to the kings and nations of the earth precisely because it speaks their language, knows their needs, and brings to a penultimate climax their search.

## Old Testament Kingship

Just as surely as the psalm in the Old Testament context is open on the general understanding of kingship in its culture, it also stands over against it in sharp distinction. The psalm is not just one more case of ancient Near Eastern royal ideology. Rather, it represents the movement in which the cultural history of kingship is being translated into the history of the coming of the messiah. It claims that in the kingship of Judah the true God is working out the true response to the question about and the quest for the power that saves. One way to identify and describe the uniqueness of the kingship about which Psalm 2 speaks is to say it had a prophetic origin, a prophetic history, and a prophetic destiny.

The kingly office in view in the second psalm had its essential definition in the promissory covenant that the Lord made with David through Nathan the prophet. When Adonai says in verse 6 of the psalm, "I have set my king on Zion, my holy hill," the declaration points to a quite specific and unique event in Israel's history. The classic text of that event, of course, is 2 Samuel 7, where David is planning to build a house for the Lord. Nathan, the prophet, receives word from the Lord that David is not to build a house—that is, a temple—for the Lord. Instead, the Lord will build a house—that is, a dynasty—for David.

In this play on words, and in the reversal in that message, lies something fundamental about Old Testament kingship. It was customary in the ancient days for kings to build temples to their patron deity. The temple and its cult was, in fact, an expression of the glory and the policy of the human king. The prophetic words shut the door on that course to David. Instead, Adonai would build David a house, a succession of heirs to come after him. The Davidic kingship must always be the expression of the power of the Lord's promise and be subordinate to its fulfillment. The permanence of that kingship would be the permanence of the promise. Wherever "son of God" was said over a Davidide in the long history of Judah, it meant that the Lord was keeping the promise. Kingship was wholly subsumed to the powerful purpose of this God. It was meant to have no policy or purpose beyond those that belonged to the Lord and that were announced by his prophets. That is why the psalm concludes not with a call to do obeisance to the king, but with a summons to the world to find in the Davidic king the occasion to acclaim the reign of the Lord.

Old Testament kingship had a prophetic history from its beginning unto its end in the sixth and fifth centuries. From David himself down to the end of his line in the exile, and the obscure revival around Zerubbabel during the restoration, prophets accompanied the long and tortured career of Old Testament kingship. Just as it began with a prophetic word, it was pursued and beset by prophets who served as messengers of the king of heaven to his regent and representative in Jerusalem. In this context we can understand Isaiah's constant going to the king to address words from the heavenly king to the earthly king about proper policy.

The record of the sustained encounter between kings and prophets is, of course, written in the books of the prophets. It is a record of judgment. The prophetic voices made it clear that there was an unbearable contradiction between the royal office that was borne by David's successors and the way they used its authority and privilege. They were both the bearers and betrayers of the calling to make it possible for their subjects to live in the reign of God. The office sustained by the promise endured, but its incumbents were swept away in the ongoing crisis worked by the one whose sole purpose, said the prophets, is his own coming kingdom.

And in the contradiction in its career, the prophetic destiny of Old Testament kingship appeared. Alongside the royal psalms and their word about the divine purpose for Judah's kings, there began to be heard the prophecy of one yet to come. "There shall come forth a shoot from the stump of Jesse, and a branch shall go out of its roots. The spirit of the Lord shall rest upon him. . . . He shall not judge by what his eyes see, or decide by what his ears hear, but with righteousness he shall judge the poor, and decide with equity for the meek of the earth. . . . The wolf shall dwell with the lamb, and the leopard shall lie down with the kid. . . . They shall not hurt or destroy in all my holy mountain, for the earth shall be full of the knowledge of the Lord as the waters cover the sea" (Isa. 11:1–9). There began to be speech about the messiah, in the broadest sense of that term. Messianic prophecy means that the promise endured where the instruments failed. Under the powerful influence of that prophecy, the royal psalms themselves came at a later stage in their history to be read as hope for the one who comes. That is, in the first part of a trajectory moving from psalms to prophets like Isaiah, the psalms predominated. Once Isaiah had been on the scene, the psalms began to be drawn into the context of prophecy itself, and to move into another genre. Within Old Testament history itself, these psalms began to be read and understood themselves as messianic prophecy. The inauguration they described awaited a candidate; the title "Son of God" hung in the air because there was no specific human historical person to whom it could be given.

## The Messianic Trajectory
## and New Testament Proclamation

When Jesus of Nazareth was baptized by John, the title was given, says the New Testament, for a final time. The Gospels tell us that heaven said to him and of him, "Son of God" (Mark 1:11 and parallels). With that designation, the background of the psalm in world history and its redefinition in prophetic history was brought to bear on him. In him, say the Gospels, the promise to David is kept, and the covenant of God maintained in force. His life, as it is portrayed, unfolds in such congruence with the purpose of God that finally, here among us humans, there is one in whom there is no disparity between the will of God and the way of his anointed. The whole human history of making kings in hope of finding the one among many whose person unites and saves and blesses, instead of alienating, betraying, exploiting—that whole history comes to rest in him. He is a human being whose life makes it possible for the rest of us to live in the reign of God. From him the rest of us can receive justice, peace, and wholeness. All that is proclaimed and announced when the Gospel records that Jesus of Nazareth began his public career under the sign of the second psalm as interpreted by the prophets.

The entire life of Jesus, from baptism to crucifixion, was his accession, his public presentation to the nations and their rulers as God's messiah. The psalm and the prophets now have a new setting in the Gospel. They are heard now, not in the palace in the midst of royal ritual, but in a ritual of repentance baptism, in which messiah takes upon his career the rubric, "Not my will, but thine." This setting for his accession is the first sign that the quest for power as the hope of salvation would receive a radically different answer in his execution of office. He will use no other power than the power of justice, faithfulness, and love. He invests and exhausts himself in them in such a way as to make their power visible in his weakness. He teaches that power separated from them becomes mere force. It destroys; it is demonic; it is rebellion against the kingdom of God. The reign of God is found alone in willing, thankful acceptance of the selflessness of justice, faithfulness, and love.

The point of this exploration can be put in this way: Christian theology can do without messianic prophecy as prediction and fulfillment. But it cannot do without the messianic trajectory to make clear what is claimed for the one who is called king, messiah, son of God. Prophecy does not tell us who the Christ is, but it does teach us what office he fulfills in the reign of God. That he carries out the office in an utterly surprising way is the surprise of the Gospels.

## Isaiah and Christian Theology Today

And where does that leave the prophet Isaiah, now that the trajectory has come to rest on Jesus of Nazareth? Is Isaiah still of use as word to the church? Well, of much use, because as a human religious community, Christians are still subject to temptations and obscurations and perversions of our confession and our theology that are structurally similar to the ones Isaiah addressed in his prophecy. Christians are tempted to reduce the role of Jesus as messiah, son of God, to a personal dimension, to speak and think of a "personal relation to Jesus," a reality isolated from the social context of life. Jesus paid it all. Sin had spread a guilty stain; he washed it white as snow. "Personal relation to Jesus" managed by a kind of heavenly divine ritual. That confidence in grace needs to be disciplined and qualified by the prophetic word. Wash yourselves. Learn to do good. Seek justice. Correct oppression.

Christians are tempted to limit the role of Jesus, messiah, king to the sphere of the church, to speak and think of a community related to Jesus in isolation from world history, to believe that what God is doing in the church is all that God is doing in the world. The church needs the prophet's vision of a glory of God that fills the whole earth. The church needs Isaiah's vision of a heavenly king with an emphasis on the word *king*. Jesus at the right hand of God does not mean that God has vacated history, or ceased, so to say, to use Assyria as the rod of God's anger. Christians are tempted to identify the reign of Jesus Messiah with their nation, their society, and his institutions, to believe that the confession "God is with us" always means a divine guarantee to sustain the structures and the institutions on which we depend, and therefore to confuse faith in God with trust in our nation, our army, our social system. That confusion is the route to pride, arrogance, idolatry of what we have made. Our reliance on our institutions needs to be chastened by Isaiah's proclamation of the Lord's day against whatever subverts the Lord's rule as ground of being and history.

Isaiah is indeed of much use to Christian theology today. Through the trajectory that passes through his prophecy we know what it means that we have Jesus as son of God. And through the words addressed to the people of God in Isaiah's prophecy our confession is chastened and corrected according to the Word of God.

# 3

# The Community
# of the
# Second Isaiah

## ROBERT R. WILSON

### The Nature of the Problem

The prophetic oracles now found in Isaiah 40—55, the work of Second Isaiah or Deutero-Isaiah, are among the most familiar in the Old Testament. They appear regularly in the church's liturgy; they are the basis of hymns and oratorios; they are among the few Old Testament lectionary readings that are actually the basis for sermons. Most preachers will dare to preach on an Old Testament text, so long as that text is from Deutero-Isaiah.

For this reason the oracles of Deutero-Isaiah are among the most dangerous in the Old Testament. They are dangerous because they are so familiar. And when a biblical text is familiar, there is a much greater danger of assuming that we know what the text actually means. One of the most common mistakes in biblical interpretation is to confuse familiarity with understanding. The only way to avoid this mistake is to study familiar texts thoroughly and to raise consciously the question of meaning at each point in the process of study. If this sort of self-conscious reading of texts is carried out honestly, then it is likely that even familiar texts will raise questions of meaning that the interpreter must answer. When these questions are answered, then the texts can be read with greater understanding. Stripped of all its mystery and jargon, exegesis is nothing but reading and rereading biblical texts and trying to answer the questions raised by the reading process. If we do this often enough, then we eventually become competent readers and perceptive interpreters, able to use the Bible in the service of the church.

To illustrate this point about the nature of interpretation, I would like to look briefly at two familiar passages from Second Isaiah. The first is the well-beloved opening of the book in chapter 40:

> Comfort, comfort my people, says your God.
> Speak tenderly to Jerusalem,
> and cry to her that her warfare is ended,
> that her iniquity is pardoned,
> that she has received from the Lord's hand
> double for all her sins. (Isa. 40:1–2)

The basic interpretive problem in these verses is not obvious to readers of the English text, but it has plagued readers of the Hebrew text for centuries. The imperatives ("comfort," "speak," "cry") are not singular imperatives and therefore cannot be addressed to the prophet. Rather they are plural imperatives and address an unidentified group, which is to be the agent of God's salvation. Who are the members of this group? Some of the answers commonly given to this question are not very satisfactory. The idea that the group is the divine council, God's advisory committee made up of lesser deities that do God's will, is unlikely, since Second Isaiah devotes several oracles to arguing that these other deities are not deities at all and in any case are totally ineffective and unable to do anything in the cosmos. Similarly, the idea that God is here addressing the entire people of Israel is unlikely, given the fact that this group is to be the agent of salvation for all of Israel. We are therefore forced to conclude that God is speaking to only a part of Israel, and it makes sense to assume that God is addressing the disciples of Second Isaiah, the group that treasured these oracles and saw itself playing an important role in realizing the prophecies that the book contains.

The second passage that I want to examine is the famous Fourth Servant Song (Isa. 52:13—53:12), which begins, "Behold, my servant shall prosper, he shall be exalted and lifted up, and shall be very high." Since New Testament times, this song has been interpreted christologically and seen as a prophecy of Jesus' redemptive suffering on the cross. With this strong christological emphasis, it has sometimes not been noticed that for six verses in the middle of the song (53:1–6), the text takes the form of a confession in which a group admits that it did not understand the meaning of the servant's suffering: "Who has believed what *we* have heard? . . . Surely he has borne *our* griefs and carried *our* sorrows." Once again we seem to be hearing from the prophet's community, which is here explaining to us the reasons for its distinctive views on suffering and salvation.

Both of these famous passages, then, point us in the direction of the Second Isaiah community and suggest that if we want to understand the words of the prophet, we must understand something of the community that collected and passed on those words to us. However, the task of reconstructing this community is not an easy one. There is almost no extrabiblical evidence on the nature of the Jewish community in Babylon at the end of the exilic period, the time from which Second Isaiah's oracles clearly come. This means that most of our information on the community must come from the Book of Isaiah itself. Yet, because there is so little evidence, there is always a danger of reconstructing a community that has no relationship to historical Israelite communities. This danger can be minimized, however, by tying the reconstruction to historical events that took place immediately before and after the exile. In these periods there are more biblical and extrabiblical data, and these can help anchor our reconstruction of the time of Second Isaiah. For the preexilic period and the early postexilic period there is some archaeological evidence that sheds light on the Israelite community, while royal inscriptions and chronicles can tell us something about the beginnings of the exile and the rise of the Persian state. For the Persian period we also have the Elephantine and Samaria papyri and the business documents from the Jewish banking house of Murashû and Sons of Nippur, and these sources give some indication of social and religious life in Israelite communities in Egypt and Babylon. For the beginning of the exilic period, we may also draw on the biblical books of Jeremiah and Ezekiel, which give some indication of Israelite society in both Jerusalem and Babylon. The Persian period is documented by Haggai, Zechariah, Ezra, and Nehemiah, and probably also Psalms and Daniel, all of which clearly discuss the reconstruction and the ideal shape of Israelite society.

We will look first, then, at the beginning of the exile, then at the period of the reconstruction (the Persian period), and finally we will turn to the task of reconstructing the community of the Second Isaiah.

ROBERT R. WILSON

# The Beginning of the Exile

*The Political Situation*

Without going into detail about political events in Judah in the years preceding the destruction of Jerusalem and the exile, we can make several generalizations about political trends during this period.[1] First, after the death of Josiah (609 B.C.E.), the political situation in Judah seems to have become increasingly unstable. During this time Judaean kings vacillated between a policy of seeking political stability through foreign alliances, either with Babylon or with Egypt, and a policy of seeking political independence. This vacillation finally led Jehoiakim of Judah to rebel against Babylon, a rebellion that was punished by the Babylonian king Nebuchadnezzar, who invaded Judah and laid siege to Jerusalem. Jehoiachin, who was king of Judah by the time of the siege, capitulated in 597 and was deported to Babylon, along with a number of palace and temple officials and artisans. The temple and palace treasuries were drained, and some of the temple vessels were either destroyed (2 Kings 24:13) or taken to Babylon (Jeremiah 27). As far as the Book of Kings is concerned, this deportation marks the beginning of the exile (2 Kings 24:1-7). The Babylonians installed Jehoiachin's uncle Zedekiah on the throne but continued to use the title "king" to refer to the imprisoned Jehoiachin. This move apparently led to disputes in Judah over the legitimacy of Zedekiah. Jeremiah's oracles from this period suggest that he recognized Zedekiah's legitimacy, as did the authors of the Book of Kings (Jer. 22:24-30; 2 Kings 24:18-20). On the other hand, Ezekiel, and perhaps others, continued to recognize Jehoiachin as king (Ezek. 1:2). In any case, Zedekiah also followed an inconsistent foreign policy under the pressure of conflicting political advice. He finally rebelled against Babylon, perhaps as part of a larger western rebellion, and was punished by a new Babylonian invasion and siege. In 587/6 Jerusalem fell. Zedekiah was taken prisoner and, at least according to Kings and Jeremiah, the city was destroyed and the temple was stripped and burned. All of the rest of the inhabitants of the city, except for some of the "poor of the land," were taken to Babylon (2 Kings 25:12). The Babylonians installed Gedaliah as governor until an internal revolt led to his death.

The political structure in Judah after this point is unclear. In Babylon,

Jews presumably continued under the direct political control of the Babylonians, although there is no indication that this control was particularly harsh. With the accession of Amel-Marduk (562), Jehoiachin was released from prison but apparently continued under house arrest. After his death, the status of the Davidic royal family in Babylon is uncertain.

The second political trend that we should note in the early exilic period is the growing debate about the legitimacy of the Davidic line. These debates began with the accession of Zedekiah and continued through the governorship of Gedaliah. It is likely that they were accompanied by parallel debates on the legitimacy and permanency of Babylonian rule. These debates are reflected in Jeremiah's reports of arguments about the length of the exile (Jeremiah 29) and about Nebuchadnezzar's place in God's plan for Israel (Jeremiah 27—28).

A final political generalization that can be made about the early exilic period is that Israel was physically dispersed in a number of different geographical areas. This is an obvious statement, but it bears repeating because of the peculiar theological slant that it will be given by certain Israelite writers. After the Babylonian invasion in 587, Jews from Jerusalem were located in colonies in Babylon and also in Egypt, where Jeremiah himself initially went, only to be condemned by Yahweh for doing so and then made to return. In addition, there is evidence that people reoccupied cities in Judah (Jer. 40:12) and that worship was revived in the temple by the time of Gedaliah (Jeremiah 41).

## The Religious Situation

The political events that occurred during the exile were accompanied by two important religious trends.[2] First, there was apparently a growing tendency for the exiles to accept some version of the Deuteronomistic explanation for the fall of Jerusalem and the exile. The Deuteronomistic History itself provides several explanations, but they all move in roughly the same direction. The History attributes the fall variously to the sins of Manasseh (2 Kings 23:26-27; 24:1-4), to the accumulated sins of the kings of Judah (implied in the formulas describing a change of reign, e.g., 2 Kings 23:32, 37; 24:9), and to the accumulated sins of all of the people (2 Kings 21:8-9, 14-15). These explanations interpenetrate in the Book of Kings, but all are variations on the basic Deuteronomistic principle that violations of God's laws will eventually be punished. Versions of these Deuteronomistic explanations for the fall were already accepted by Jeremiah, who held both the kings (Jeremiah 36) and the people (e.g., Jer. 14:1—15:4) responsible for the catastrophe. Ezekiel accepted his own variant of this theology, arguing that the exile was due to the accumulated sins of the people (Ezekiel 16, 23, 20) and to the political blunders of the kings (Ezekiel 17). For this reason, the destruction of Jerusalem became inevitable, according to Ezekiel, and salvation would be available only to individuals who repented and then consciously worked to live righteously within their exilic communities (Ezekiel 18).

Still unresolved in this Deuteronomistic explanation was the question of the finality of the exile. The Deuteronomistic History and Jeremiah sometimes speak as if God's rejection of Israel and Jerusalem is total and final (2 Kings 24:3; 21:10-15; Jer. 14:1—15:14; 17:1-4). Yet Jeremiah also prophesies a long but limited exile, with a chance for future restoration (Jeremiah 27—29; 30—32). As the exile continued, one might suspect that debates about this issue would have intensified.

A second important religious trend was a growing debate about the identity of the true Israel. This question is first reflected in Ezekiel, where the prophet reports an exclusivistic Jerusalemite claim to the land of Israel and the divine promises that go with the land. Ezekiel 11:14-21 reports that those who were left in Jerusalem after the first deportation were saying that the Babylonian exiles were no longer a part of the people of God, part of the true Israel: "Son of man, your brethren, even your brethren, your own kin, the whole house of Israel, all of them, are those of whom the inhabitants of Jerusalem have said, 'They have gone far from the Lord; to us this land is given for a possession.'" The argument is apparently that either because of physical separation or because they are being punished for their sins, the exiles are no longer part of Israel. The oracle goes on to refute this claim and argues precisely the opposite point. The exiles are the ones called "the whole house of Israel," and God claims to have taken up temporary residence with them in exile and promises to bring them back to the land, where *they* will clearly be the people of God. From Ezekiel's perspective, the remaining Jerusalemites have misread the historical situation. The judgment against Israel has not been completed in the first deportation; it has just begun. The final judgment—that is, the destruction of Jerusalem and the slaughter or deportation of its inhabitants—is inevitable. God has in fact already deserted the city (Ezekiel 8—11) and begun the process of destruction that will end in a Babylonian victory. Then Ezekiel's fellow exiles will return and become the new Israelite community.

A similar debate over the identity of the true Israel is reflected in a curious set of passages in Jeremiah. These passages, which seem to be from a late level of the Jeremiah tradition, imply that the only survivors of the second deportation are the Babylonian exiles.[3] The reader gets the curious impression that the destroyed Jerusalem is devoid of inhabitants. Only the Babylonian exiles are the remnant of Israel. This situation is first given theological coloring in Jeremiah's vision of the good and bad figs which are brought to the temple and placed before Yahweh (Jer. 24:1-10). The bad figs are identified with Zedekiah, the remnant in Jerusalem, and the exiles in Egypt, while the good figs are those who are in exile in Babylon. Only the latter exiles are the true Israel that will be brought back to the land. All of the others will be destroyed. This notion of the supremacy of the Babylonian exiles is reinforced in Jeremiah 41 in a series of devastating judgment oracles against the Judahite remnant in Egypt. It is probably safe to assume that debates about the identity of the true Israel continued during the later exilic period and that the argument that the future of Israel lay in Babylon was particularly popular among the exiles there.

## The End of the Exile

### The Political and Historical Situation

Many of the same political trends that existed in the early exilic period seem to have continued into the beginning of the period of the restoration.[4] First, political instability continued in Babylon during the last days of the Babylonian empire, and news of the progressive Persian advance toward the Babylonian heartland must have caused much uncertainty about the political changes that might occur under Persian rule. The coming of the Persians might have also fueled speculation about a possible return of Jewish exiles to Jerusalem.

Second, once the possibility of return became a reality, debates about the polity of the restored Israelite state seem to have continued. Ezra and Nehemiah seem to show a willingness to recognize Persian political authority, but the limits of Israelite political authority remained uncertain. Particularly problematic was the question of the restoration of the Davidic monarchy. Haggai 2:20-23 seems to advocate the enthronement of the Davidide Zerubbabel, while Ezra 3 and Zech. 4:6–10 recognize his royal status but stop short of arguing for a reinstatement of the monarchy.

Third, the Persian period seems to have been one of social stability and assimilation for the Jewish exiles in Babylon. Evidence on this point for the later Persian period comes from the Murashû texts, which show that some Jews were well integrated into the economic life of Nippur. Some of the Jews apparently adopted Babylonian names, although the extent of their actual assimilation to Babylonian culture is uncertain. The problem of assimilation is reflected also in the so-called court tales of Daniel 1, 3, and 6, which at their earliest levels seem concerned with the question of how far assimilation into a foreign culture may proceed before one's Jewish identity is threatened. Ezra and Nehemiah were also concerned with this problem. The authors were embarrassed by the reluctance of some Jews to return to Jerusalem and by the existence of mixed marriages among the exiles who did return.

Fourth, there is no indication of Persian persecution early in the Persian period, although it is unclear how far back into the exilic period this toleration of the Jews can be retrojected. However, the degree of Jewish economic integration into the Persian period suggests that life under the Babylonians was not harsh for those willing to recognize the political authority of the state. This picture also agrees with the one that can be deduced from Daniel 1, 3, and 6, where routine persecution of Jews does not seem to be in the picture. However, the limits of Babylonian and Persian tolerance are unclear.

Finally, the early Persian period seems to have witnessed a resurgence of Jewish nationalism, at least among those groups that actually returned to the land. In Ezra and Nehemiah the Persians are portrayed as being tolerant of this sort of nationalism as long as it did not lead to political instability. The attitude of the Babylonians toward nationalism in the late exilic period is uncertain.

## The Religious Situation

Some of the same issues that caused debate in the early exilic period also were controversial at the beginning of the Persian period.[5] The Deuteronomistic point of view still seems to have been the dominant one, but at least some groups had rejected the notion that exile was to be a permanent state of affairs. However, debates over the identity of the true

Israel continued. For Ezra and Nehemiah, the true Israel was certainly the exiles in Babylon, and specifically the Babylonian exiles who actually returned. The returning exiles described in Ezra-Nehemiah rejected participation in the reestablished cult by people already living in the land of Israel, whoever they may have been, and apparently did not recognize the legitimacy of Israelites living in Egypt. These narrow views were presumably not shared by Egyptian Israelites, such as those in the community at Elephantine, or by Jews who had remained in Palestine after 587. Both of these groups would have certainly seen themselves as legitimate worshipers of Yahweh and would have disputed the claims of the returning Babylonian exiles that supported the views of Ezra and Nehemiah. Arguments about the nature of the true Israel also helped to fuel disputes about the nature of restored worship and particularly about the shape and orientation of the rebuilt temple. On this point there were arguments even among the returning Babylonian exiles.

To summarize: The evidence from the beginning of the exilic period and from the Persian period suggests that the late exilic period, the period of Second Isaiah, was a period of political and religious controversy over the appropriate structure for a religious community in exile. There seems to have been a general acceptance of the Deuteronomistic theology, although its interpretation was debated. The degree of permissible assimilation was discussed, and along with these discussions went questions about the possibility of return and about the nature of the reconstructed state. Above all, there were questions about the nature and identity of the true Israel.

This general summary of political and religious conditions during the time of the Second Isaiah can provide a helpful background against which to examine the book in order to see what clues it might provide about the nature of the prophet's community. A comprehensive reconstruction of this community is not permitted because of the scarcity of the evidence, but a few generalizations are at least possible.

## The Community of Second Isaiah

### The Social Location of the Community

The literature produced by the Second Isaiah community suggests two important features of the group's location within the social spectrum of the Babylonian exiles. First, the group clearly saw itself as a minority within the exilic community. An indication of this minority status can be seen in the tone of the book, which makes heavy use of the language of exhortation. The reader gets the clear sense that the group is trying to convince its audience of a theological and political position that most of the exiles do not accept. The rhetoric of persuasion permeates the literature, a fact that suggests that the Second Isaiah community was arguing for a minority point of view.[6]

Even clearer indications of the community's minority status can be seen in the references to persecution that appear periodically in the book. These references are usually taken to be allusions to oppression by the Babylonian authorities, but this explanation is unlikely, given the generally benign nature of the interaction between Babylonians and Israelites that characterized the exile. Rather, a more plausible explanation for the references is to assume that they are related to the friction caused by the community's unsuccessful attempts to convince other exiles of its description of the way that God intends to bring about a return to the land.

It is difficult to isolate the precise causes of this friction, but the literary contexts in which the references to persecution appear suggest at least two possibilities. One component of the community's view that would certainly have drawn criticism from other exiles was the group's claim that the Persian king, Cyrus, was God's anointed ruler who would govern all of the Near East, including Israel (Isa. 45:1–7). The community thus rejected any hope of restoring a native Israelite to David's throne and envisioned a restored Israelite state in which all political authority was to be exercised by the Persian government. Although other exiles would eventually come to accept this point of view (cf. Ezra 7:25–26; Neh. 6:1–19), it would have been controversial at a time when nationalistic hopes were still strongly held by many of the exiles. The Second Isaiah community's political views may thus help to explain why it felt compelled to defend itself against its opponents:

> Woe to him who strives with his Maker,
> an earthen vessel with the potter.
> Does the clay say to him who fashions it,
> "What are you making"?
> or "Your work has no handles"?
> Woe to him who says to a father,

"What are you begetting?"
or to a woman, "With what
are you in travail?"
Thus says the Lord,
the Holy One of Israel,
and his Maker:
"Will you question me
about my children
or command me concerning
the work of my hands?" (Isa. 45:9-11)

The most explicit references to persecution appear in Isaiah 51, where the text suggests a second reason that the community may have been persecuted. At least by the time these oracles were written, the community apparently considered itself to be an elite group which God had set apart from the rest of the exiles for a particular task. Like many members of persecuted minority groups, the members of the Second Isaiah community seem to have seen themselves as the only remaining bearers of the true faith. In the exilic context, this view would have amounted to a claim to be the true Israel, the Israel which was truly God's servant. In Second Isaiah's prophetic oracles, God addresses the community as "you who know righteousness" and as the "people in whose heart is my law" (Isa. 51:7). In contrast, the community's persecutors are described as those who "have forgotten the Lord, your Maker" (51:13). Such an exclusivistic claim on the part of the community could well have encouraged opposition by other exilic groups who themselves laid claim to being God's elect. In the face of this opposition, the Second Isaiah community is exhorted not to be discouraged by persecution and to remember that God's salvation is eternal while persecution is fleeting (51:7-8, 12). The community is promised speedy deliverance from its oppressed state (51:14) and is reassured of its special place in God's plan for Israel's salvation (51:15-16). In spite of opposition, the community will ultimately triumph and accomplish the task that God has sent it to do. At the same time, its opponents will be shown to be liars and fools:

Thus says the Lord, your Redeemer,
.......................................
who frustrates the omens of liars,
and makes fools of diviners;
who turns wise men back,
and makes their knowledge foolish;

who confirms the word of his servant,
and performs the counsel of his messengers;
who says of Jerusalem, "She shall be inhabited,"
and of the cities of Judah, "They shall be built,
and I will raise up their ruins;"
who says to the deep, "Be dry,
I will dry up your rivers;"
who says of Cyrus, "He is my shepherd,
and he shall fulfill all my purpose,
saying of Jerusalem, 'She shall be built,'
and of the temple, 'Your foundations
shall be laid.'" (Isa. 44:24–28)

In addition to the fact that the community of the Second Isaiah was a minority within the larger group of exiled Israelites, the texts also suggest a second feature of the community's social location. The Second Isaiah community had strong links with priestly tradition. Four lines of evidence point in this direction.[7] First, scholars have often noted theological links between Second Isaiah and the priestly layers of the Pentateuch, although the significance of these links has not always been recognized. Both biblical sources share similar traditions about creation, the period of the ancestors, and the exodus. Both also share the characteristic Jerusalemite belief that God dwells in Israel in the form of the divine glory (*kābôd*).[8] This theology of the nature of God's presence is particularly prominent in priestly circles. It is found throughout the priestly portions of the Pentateuch and plays a major role in the writings of the prophet Ezekiel, who was an exiled Zadokite priest. Finally, it is present in the oracles of First Isaiah, whose priestly status cannot be demonstrated but who was a representative of the royal Jerusalemite theology.

A second link between Second Isaiah and priestly tradition is a shared vocabulary. Both sources tend to use the same terms to discuss technical and theological issues, and at the same time these terms are not used by writers from other Israelite theological and literary traditions.

Third, Second Isaiah makes extensive use of a literary form that scholars traditionally call the "salvation oracle." This type of oracle is usually thought to have been used in Israel's cult, where it was delivered by a priest to worshipers who had brought a complaint or a request to the temple. After the worshiper presented the complaint, the priest responded with a salvation oracle, assuring the sufferer that God would hear the complaint and grant relief.[9]

Finally, the community of the Second Isaiah shared with priestly tradition a deep concern for the cultic purity of the restored Jerusalem and the people who would be allowed to enter it. This concern, to which the Priestly writers and Ezekiel also devote much attention, can be seen most clearly in oracles directed to Zion, the servant city, and to the members of the community, who are to play a special role in Zion's redemption:

> Awake, awake, put on your strength, O Zion;
> put on your beautiful garments, O Jerusalem, the holy city;
> for there shall no more come into you
> the uncircumcised and the unclean.
> ........................................
> Depart, depart, go out thence,
> touch no unclean thing;
> go out from the midst of her, purify yourselves,
> you who bear the vessels of the Lord. (Isa. 52:1, 11)

As God's servant, the newly purified community is to leave exile and return to the land, bringing with it the temple vessels which were removed from Jerusalem by the Babylonians. Once in Jerusalem, the community is to purify the entire city, not just the temple itself, and restore appropriate worship.

These concerns for cultic purity and for the sanctity of Jerusalem were apparently shared by many priestly groups in the exilic and postexilic periods (cf. Ezekiel 40—48; Zech. 14:20-21), although the groups often differed in their views of the degree of purity which was to be maintained. It is impossible to identify with any certainty the specific priestly group to which members of the Second Isaiah community belonged. The characteristic Zadokite priestly notions of purity, which are reflected in Ezekiel 40—48, do not seem to be present in Second Isaiah, and the Deuteronomistic views usually associated with Levitical priests are not present either. It may be that the community represented some branch of the Aaronide priesthood, but further research must be done on this question before any conclusions can be reached.

*The Religious Perspective of the Community*

Although Second Isaiah provides only a few hints about the social location of the community that produced these oracles, the book is much more explicit about the religious and political program that the community advocated. There are essentially four points to this program. First, as we have already noted, the community advocated a return to Zion and a restoration of life in the land. Against other exiles who argued that such a return was impossible or unnecessary, the Second Isaiah group argued that God required such a return and that God was powerful enough to make the return a reality. Other deities and secular rulers were powerless to oppose God's will, and even the natural forces of the cosmos would cooperate in bringing about the return of the Israelites. Many of the oracles in the book underline this point and seek to give new hope to exiles who had become convinced that God had permanently rejected them. At the same time that the community exhorted the exiles to return to the land, however, it also accepted the political rule of the Persians. Cyrus is called both "shepherd" (Isa. 44:28) and "the anointed of Yahweh" (45:1), titles traditionally used in Israel to refer to the Davidic king. There is no evidence that the community expected the restoration of the Davidic monarchy, and it presumably rejected the attempts of Davidides who sought to reclaim the throne.

Second, the Second Isaiah community saw itself as God's servants, the human agents through whom God would accomplish the divine plan for history, a plan which involved a return to the land, the establishment of a theocratic state with Jerusalem as its center, and the transformation of Jerusalem into a priestly city from which the Torah of Yahweh could go forth to the rest of Israel and ultimately to the rest of the world. The details of this scenario are presented most comprehensively in the famous opening verses of Isaiah 40. The oracle begins with an address to the community, which is instructed to comfort God's people and the representative Israelite city, Jerusalem, which like the people themselves has been mourning and suffering in exile (40:1-2). The community is then told to prepare a way for Yahweh to return to the deserted city along with the exiles from Babylon (40:3-5). God's word of promise will ultimately be established, and Zion itself, as God's servant-messenger, is called to give to the rest of the cities of Judah the glad news of Yahweh's return (40:8-11). When the community returns to Jerusalem as Yahweh's agents of salvation, then the newly energized city can take upon itself the role of God's servant and function as an agent of salvation for the rest of the nation (52:1-12; cf. 2:2-3).

The third point in the community's program was a belief that the Babylonian exiles in general and the members of the community itself in particular were the true Israel. Originally the community may have believed that God would allow only the Babylonian exiles to return to the land and would reject Israelites living in other parts of the world (48:20–22; 43:14). However, the community later broadened this exclusivistic notion and held that all Israelites, and even all nations, would come to know Yahweh's salvation (43:1–7).

The final point in the community's program was a limited acceptance of the Deuteronomistic explanation for the fall of Jerusalem and the exile. The community admitted that the exile occurred because God punished the people for their past sins, so that in a real sense the people were the direct cause of their own suffering (42:23–25). However, it is important to note that the community accepted this point of view only as a historical explanation and did not make it into an explanation for all suffering. Although the group was concerned about the suffering that it had endured in exile and about the suffering of Zion itself, it was willing to attribute to Yahweh only the suffering that the people and the city had earned because of its sin. For *undeserved* suffering the community developed a different and much more influential explanation, an explanation perhaps inspired by the priestly notion of substitutionary atonement. The community understanding of undeserved suffering is spelled out most clearly in Isa. 52:13—53:12, the so-called Fourth Servant Song. In this autobiographical passage the community confesses how it came to understand the fate of a single individual, presumably one of the members of the community who had suffered and perhaps even died. Beginning with a statement of their faith that this individual will ultimately be exalted by Yahweh, the members of the community confess that they first interpreted the individual's fate according to standard Deuteronomistic theological principles. Because this person was suffering, he must have done something to deserve the punishment that God was inflicting upon him:

> He was despised and rejected by men;
> a man of sorrow, and acquainted with grief;
> and as one from whom men hide their faces
> he was despised, and we esteemed him not.
> ................................................
> We esteemed him stricken,
> smitten by God and afflicted. (53:3-4)

However, the community then admits that it had misunderstood the

ROBERT R. WILSON

cause of the individual's suffering. The real explanation was far more extraordinary and difficult to believe than the Deuteronomistic explanation that the community had originally accepted:

Who has believed what we have heard?
And to whom has the arm of the Lord been revealed? (53:1)

In fact the individual was suffering vicariously for the benefit of the rest of the community:

Surely he has borne our griefs
and carried our sorrows;
..............................
He was wounded for our transgressions,
he was bruised for our iniquities;
upon him was the chastisement that made us whole,
and with his stripes we are healed.
All we like sheep have gone astray;
we have turned every one to his own way;
and the Lord has laid upon him
the iniquity of us all. (53:4-6)

This new understanding of the true cause of unmerited suffering not only helped group members to comprehend the fate of this one individual but also provided an interpretive key that helped them unlock the mystery of their own undeserved suffering. They had done nothing to deserve the persecution that the other exiles had visited upon them. Rather, the Second Isaiah community was suffering vicariously for the sins of their fellow exiles. This suffering would ultimately be redemptive for all of Israel and would eventually result in the exaltation of the community to the status of God's elect. The same principle could be applied to the sufferings of Zion itself. To be sure, Zion had originally sinned and had been punished through deserved destruction and exile. However, those sins had now been atoned for, and the city was enduring an extra, undeserved measure of suffering. "She has received from the Lord's hand double for all her sins" (40:2). The group could now understand this undeserved suffering, this unexpectedly long exile, not as a failure of God's justice but as a redemptive act on the part of the servant city. The city had suffered for the sake of the people, and that suffering would end in the restoration of the city to its former status as Yahweh's own chosen city, from which the divine redemptive word would go forth to all nations (40:9-11; 52:1-10).

68

## THE COMMUNITY OF THE SECOND ISAIAH

Using the evidence of the texts themselves, the community of Second Isaiah can be reconstructed with reasonable clarity, and this reconstruction in turn helps us to read in a more sophisticated way the texts that the community treasured. Although the prophet's disciples were destined to see their priestly reform program fail in many of its details, they were able to forge from their traditions and their common experience a sustaining vision of God that helped them to survive the trauma of exile, and they gave to the world an understanding of human suffering that would transform the experiences of later Jewish and Christian communities. The Second Isaiah community thus became a model that other communities would do well to follow.

## NOTES

1. For a more thorough discussion of the political events surrounding the fall of Jerusalem, see Bustenay Oded, "Judah and the Exile," in *Israelite and Judaean History*, ed. John H. Hayes and J. Maxwell Miller (Philadelphia: Westminster Press, 1977), 435–88; and John Bright, *A History of Israel,* 3d ed. (Philadelphia: Westminster Press, 1981), 310–39.

2. For a more thorough discussion of religious conditions during the exile, see Peter R. Ackroyd, *Exile and Restoration* (Philadelphia: Westminster Press, 1968); and Ralph W. Klein, *Israel in Exile: A Theological Interpretation* (Philadelphia: Fortress Press, 1979).

3. For a more thorough discussion of this point of view, see Karl-Friedrich Pohlmann, *Studien zum Jeremiabuch* (Göttingen: Vandenhoeck & Ruprecht, 1978).

4. For a more thorough discussion of the history of the Persian period, see Bright, *History of Israel*, 341–402; Geo Widengren, "The Persian Period," in *Israelite and Judaean History*, ed. Hayes and Miller, 489–538; W. D. Davies and Louis Finkelstein, eds., *The Cambridge History of Judaism: Volume One: Introduction, The Persian Period* (Cambridge: At the University Press, 1984); and Ephraim Stern, *Material Culture of the Land of the Bible in the Persian Period 538–332 B.C.* (Warminster: Aris & Phillips, 1982).

5. For a more thorough discussion of religious conditions in the Persian period, see Ackroyd, *Exile and Restoration;* Klein, *Israel in Exile;* and Peter R. Ackroyd, "Archaeology, Politics and Religion: The Persian Period" (The Inaugural Lecture of the Walter G. Williams Lectureship in Old Testament; Denver: Iliff School of Theology, 1982).

6. For a detailed treatment of this feature of the book, see Yehoshua Gitay, *Prophecy and Persuasion: A Study of Isaiah 40—48* (Bonn: Linguistica Biblica, 1981).

7. For a thorough discussion of the linguistic and theological links between Second Isaiah and priestly tradition, see Carroll Stuhlmueller, *Creative Redemption in Deutero-Isaiah* (Rome: Biblical Institute Press, 1970); and Andreas Eitz, "Studien zum Verhältnis von Priesterschrift und Deuterojesaja" (Inaugural-Dissertation, Heidelberg, 1969).

8. For a discussion of this motif, see Stuhlmueller, *Creative Redemption*, 95–98; and Tryggve N. D. Mettinger, *The Dethronement of Sabaoth: Studies in the Shem and Kabod Theologies* (Lund: C. W. K. Gleerup, 1982), 80–134.

9. This type of oracle has been analyzed in detail in Joachim Begrich, "Das priesterliche Heilsorakel," *Zeitschrift für die alttestamentliche Wissenschaft* 52 (1934): 81–92. Cf. the later discussions of Stuhlmueller, *Creative Redemption*, 19–28; and Edgar W. Conrad, "The Community as King in Second Isaiah," in *Understanding the Word: Essays in Honor of Bernhard W. Anderson*, ed. James T. Butler et al. (Sheffield: JSOT Press, 1985), 99–111.

# 4

# Second Isaiah: An Evangelical Rereading of Communal Experience*

## WALTER BRUEGGEMANN

We are more likely to be attracted to 2 Isaiah than to Jeremiah, certainly more drawn to it than to Ezekiel. It is buoyant literature of hope exquisitely expressed. "Second Isaiah" refers to Isaiah 40—55, a literature set deep in the Babylonian exile, commonly dated to 540 B.C.E., just as the Babylonian empire was about to collapse in the face of rising Persian power.

Powerful as it is, the literature of 2 Isaiah cannot be understood and cannot be used without linkage to Jeremiah and to Ezekiel. Second Isaiah, as Handel has made so powerfully clear, is marvelously filled with promises. But those promises are addressed only to people in exile who have seen the city fall (40:2) and have suffered the loss of their entire world of faith. The power of the hope found in this poetry is not likely to be felt without the conflict of Jeremiah and without the toughness of Ezekiel. The promises are not available to us or effective for us while we are people who cling to the old city and to old organizations of reality. To use the poetry of homecoming without the prior literature of *exile* is an offer of cheap grace. It is important that the "new thing" of 2 Isaiah comes after a long season of exilic discontent. That discontent, failure, and grief are evidenced either in the poet quoting what must have been said (or thought) by exiles, or in the refutation of their complaints from which we may deduce the expression of doubt and grief:

---

*Appears as chap. 5 in Walter Brueggemann, *Hopeful Imagination: Prophetic Voices in Exile* (Philadelphia: Fortress Press, 1986), under the title "Second Isaiah—Homecoming to a New Home."

Why do you say, O Jacob,
and speak, O Israel,
"My way is hid from the Lord,
and my right is disregarded by my God"? (Isa. 40:27)

But Zion said, "The Lord has forgotten me." (49:14; au. trans.)

Is my hand shortened, that it cannot redeem?
Or have I no power to deliver? (50:2)

On the basis of literary genre, historical allusions, and theological for-
mulations, the literature of Isaiah 40—55 has been judged to be distinct
from Isaiah 1—39 (1 Isaiah). Its context is apparently the Babylonian
exile of the sixth century B.C.E. The poetry of these chapters is concerned
with the end of the Babylonian empire (cf. Isaiah 46—47) and the rise of
Persia under Cyrus (cf. 44:28; 45:1). Cyrus practiced a benevolent imperial policy that permitted deported groups to return to their homeland.
As Jeremiah saw Babylon under Nebuchadnezzar as an agent of Yahweh's judgment, so 2 Isaiah sees Persia under Cyrus as an agent of Yahweh's restorative action. The idea of being rescued by a Gentile must
have been radical enough to evoke serious resistance (see 45:9-13 in
response to such resistance).

More recently scholars have begun to question the notion that Isaiah
40—55 is a literature that can be treated apart from Isaiah 1—39.[1] It has
been noticed afresh that chapters 40—55 have important and intentional
connections to chapters 1—39 and that this relationship in the Book of
Isaiah is more than an accidental juxtaposition. Rather, it is suggested,
the "new thing" of God's deliverance (cf. Isa. 43:18-19) is intended precisely as a countertheme to God's judgment in chapters 1—39. These two
scholarly positions, critical and canonical, are now in tension among
scholars, with no resolution in sight. Our particular treatment of Isaiah
40—55 here can be sustained in either scholarly judgment, because we
appeal to the imaginative practice of the poetry and not to historical
facticity. Our exposition posits a theological situation of exile and new-
ness, without respect to specific historical location.

### Three Metaphors for "Rereading"
### Israel's Life

The poetry of 2 Isaiah is shaped by powerful poetic metaphors.
The social, historical setting for this poetry is exile. The poet thus

must be heard through the metaphor of *exile*. The words grow out of and are aimed at an alienated community (cf. Psalm 137). The central fact of the community of 2 Isaiah was the power and authority of Babylonian definitions of reality (cf. Isa. 39:1-8). Babylonian cultural voices in many ways shaped Jews just as they succeeded in shaping everything and everyone else in the empire. In as many ways as possible, it was the ideological intent of the empire to talk Jews out of Jewish perceptions of reality and into Babylonian definitions of reality, to define life in terms of Babylonian values, Babylonian hopes, and Babylonian fears. Jeremiah (25:9; 27:6) had judged Babylonian triumph to be the will of Yahweh, but in the new circumstance and new generation of 2 Isaiah, it is now Yahweh's will to have Israel depart from the alien empire (Isa. 52:11-12). God will gather the displaced (43:5), releasing them from Babylon (43:14). Yahweh will send Cyrus to accomplish the release of this displaced community (45:1-4), in order that Israel may come home with joy to make a new beginning in restored Jerusalem (54:12-14).

The metaphor of Babylonian exile was used by Martin Luther who argued that the gospel had been exiled in his time by the Babylonian captivity of the Roman Catholic Church.[2] Thus he intended exile to be a very harsh metaphor to suggest that the shaping influence of the Roman Catholic Church of his time was alien and hostile to the gospel. We do not need to pursue Luther's particular handling of the metaphor to see its potential for our own interpretive situation.[3]

As we try to appropriate the metaphor of exile, we may wish to think about the church and ask if we are in exile. The metaphor of exile may be useful to American Christians as a way of understanding the social context of the church in American culture. The exile of the contemporary American church is that we are bombarded by definitions of reality that are fundamentally alien to the gospel, definitions of reality that come from the military-industrial-scientific empire, which may be characterized as "consumer capitalism."[4] In a variety of ways the voice of this empire wants to reshape our values, fears, and dreams in ways that are fundamentally opposed to the voice of the gospel.

There are, of course, many American Christians who do not know this and do not believe it. It is not known or believed because they sense no abrasion between those cultural values and evangelical values (values derived from the gospel). Such American Christians proceed on the assumption that our society is fundamentally Christian and that there is a ready and comfortable interface between Christianity and those cultural values. If that view be held (which I think is wrong), then the exilic literature makes little sense or has no direct pertinence. That is an important issue for the way in which our argument proceeds. If the church is in fact in exile, as I believe it to be, then to try to do ministry as if we are practicing imperial religion robs us of energy. My own judgment is that honestly facing exile as our real situation generates energy for imaginative and faithful living. Exile in the ancient world or in our own situation is not an obvious, flat, social fact. It is a decision one must make. It is a very specific, self-conscious reading of social reality. There must have been many Jews in Babylon in the sixth century who settled in, made it home, assimilated, and did not perceive themselves as exiles. Such accommodation is a possible stance for faith, in ancient Babylon or in contemporary America. I should only say that such a pragmatic decision against exile excludes one from the imaginative field of this literature of exile. "Exile" is not simply a geographical fact, but also a theological decision.

My interpretive analogue from 2 Isaiah is aimed at the American situation, where I find the claims of the gospel not hospitably received. One can make the same exilic reading of the church community in the totalitarian context of Eastern Europe. Quite clearly, the church there is a community in an alien and hostile environment. I do not propose the church context of Eastern Europe as a preferable alternative to our own, for the gospel is rejected by the dominant values there as well. But I suggest our task as pastors and Christians is not to use our energy on those more distant issues but to face the faith situation of exile as it concerns us where our ministry is given. Our American faith situation may be more seductive than such oppressive contexts because the reading of exile is not so unambiguous for us. I proceed here, however, on the assumption that the notion of the Christian church in American culture being in exile is a correct reading of the situation. I do so strategically in order to make a case from this literature. I do so because that is in fact my assessment of our social situation. In the argument that follows, then, I assume that our situation as American Christians may be treated as a very rough parallel to that of Jews in the Babylonian empire. In both the Babylonian and American contexts, there are many dimensions of life to be affirmed and appropriated. But in both the fundamental perceptions and values are in opposition to the faith of Israel.

Second Isaiah's poetry is organized around the metaphor of homecoming, a metaphor that makes sense only to those who read their context as exile. The whole of this poetry is preoccupied with one overriding proclamation: *homecoming*. Thus Isa. 40:1–11 envisions a great procession led by Yahweh as exiled Jews come home. Yahweh will gather into the land of Zion all those who had been scattered in exile (43:5–6). The watchmen on the walls of desolate Jerusalem watch with eager longing for some news of a fresh possibility. When they receive word of Yahweh's triumphant return from exile, they rejoice (52:7–10). As a result, the fallen city will be rebuilt (44:28; 54:11–12). There will be a rebuilding and a gathering (49:17–18). Judah had been hopeless but now will be safely at home. It is for this reason that new songs of joy, celebration, and buoyancy can now be sung (42:10–17).

By the power and the mercy of God, this community of faith will very soon be led back to the "holy land" where the values of the Torah tradition are not resisted but in fact received and practiced as normative and true. It is a deep yearning in this faith community of exile to be in the only place where those values are presumed. For good reason that place is "home."

The use of these two metaphors, *exile* and *homecoming*, is an act of remarkable evangelical imagination. The *homecoming* metaphor makes sense only where the metaphor of *exile* has been accepted as true. Second Isaiah's poetry of homecoming is precisely imaginative poetry which liberates. It is not based in political analysis, though the poet obviously knew what was going on in his world. It is an imaginative act of speech that intends to evoke reality and lead this community out beyond their present situation. The poetry is grounded in a theological conviction of God's sovereignty (40:9–11; 52:7). It is also informed by political analysis (45:1–6). The poetry, as such, is not explained either by theological conviction or by political analysis, but by an inventive, creative act of poetry that means to speak this community out beyond present circumstance by the force of the poetic word, which is offered as the fresh decree of God's own mouth (45:11; 55:10–11). I am assuming that the power of language to shape reality and not just describe reality is true for us as well as for this poet. The poet does not only describe a new social reality but wills it. The very art of poetic speech establishes new reality. Public speech, the articulation of alternative scenarios of reality, is one of the key acts of a ministry among exiles.[5]

The exiles were securely and perhaps despondently exiles. They could not imagine any other status. They accepted Babylonian definitions of reality, not because they were convinced, but because no alternatives were available. These Babylonian claims seemed as if they would endure to perpetuity (47:7, 8, 10). This exiled community was in despair because it accepted Babylonian definitions of reality and did not know any others were available. That is, they were hopeless. They did not believe Yahweh could counter Babylon (49:14; 50:2).

It was the peculiar vocation of 2 Isaiah to construct poetic scenarios of alternative reality outside the prosaic control of the empire. These fresh alternatives liberated Jewish exiles to think differently, act differently, speak differently, and sing differently. In the end Babylonian definitions of reality lost their absoluteness and their authority because this poetry served to subvert the absoluteness.

The Babylonian gods have been dethroned by the poetry:

Bel bows down, Nebo stoops . . .
They stoop, they bow down together,
  They cannot save the burden,
  but themselves go into captivity. (Isa. 46:1–2)

The very gods who authorized captivity for Judah are now themselves destined to the same fate. As the gods are subverted in this poetry, so the inflated claims of the empire are also emptied in humiliation:

Come down and sit in the dust,
  O virgin daughter of Babylon;
sit on the ground without a throne,
  O daughter of the Chaldeans! (Isa. 47:1)

The poetry articulates an empire that has failed and is humiliated. It need no longer be feared or trusted. Freedom to go home began to well up in this community. The poet offers scenarios of a triumphant procession on its way home in joy and power (40:1–11; 43:4–7; 45:14–17).

The triggering of this new social possibility is a poetic articulation of an alternative social reality that at first lives only in the mind and heart of the poet but begins to form a community ready in various ways to disengage from the dominant reality. That was the ministry of this poet in exile. Our ministry in our exile requires the same clarity and courage that 2 Isaiah had which gave energy and freedom in his exile.

## Imagination Toward What Will Be

The practice of such *poetic imagination* is the most subversive, redemptive act that a leader of a faith community can undertake in the midst of exiles. This work of poetic alternative in the long run is more crucial than one-on-one pastoral care or the careful implementation of institutional goals. That is because the work of poetic imagination holds the potential of unleashing a community of power and action that finally will not be contained by any imperial restrictions and definitions of reality.

1. Second Isaiah is the supreme example of liberated poetic imagination in the Old Testament. We are so familiar with the words that we fail to note how the poetic rendering evokes an entirely different perception of reality. The poetry is not derived from external historical experience. The poetry cannot be adequately explained by observing that Babylonian power would eventually succumb to the rise of Persia under Cyrus. Poetry here is not simply code language for political events.

Rather, the poet appeals to the old memories and affirmations in an astonishing way to jar the perceptual field of Israel and to cause a wholly new discernment of reality. The poetry opens with a heavenly scenario in which the voices of members of the divine council fashion a new proclamation (40:1-8). This is immediately followed by a rhetorical act of enthronement (40:9) in which Yahweh, who had seemed weak, is now placed triumphantly at the head of a grand procession (40:10-11).

The poetry does not describe what is happening. Rather, it evokes images and invites perceptions in Israel that were not available apart from this poetry. The poetry is not aimed first of all at external conduct, as though the poet expected people immediately to start packing for travel. Rather, the poetry cuts underneath behavior to begin to transform the self-image, communal image, and image of historical possibility. The rhetoric works to deabsolutize imperial modes of reality, so that fresh forms of communal possibility can be entertained. Second Isaiah's dramatic sensitivity constructs worlds of gods in court (41:21-29), rulers being summoned by Yahweh (44:24-28; 45:1-5), dragons being defeated (51:9), cities being rebuilt (54:11-14). The outcome of such poetry is hope. Hope makes community possible on the way out of the empire.

The poet creates with incredible scope and vividness. One can hear the chains rattling and the nations yielding. One can conjure Cyrus acting in liberation and Babylonians cowering in subjugation. One can hear the ecstatic sounds of Sarah now with child (54:1–3), and the flood waters of Noah subsiding (54:9–11).

2. Jesus' way of teaching through parables was such a pastoral act of prophetic imagination in which he invited his community of listeners out beyond the visible realities of Roman law and the ways in which Jewish law had grown restrictive in his time.[6] Like 2 Isaiah, Jesus does this precisely out of the tradition itself. It is clear that he tells parables consistent with the rabbinic tradition, but his parables serve to conjure alternative social reality. They are specific, but they are open-ended. The listener, when the story is ended, is not instructed and does not know what to do. The stories intend to characterize an alternative society which he calls "kingdom of God,"[7] but the stories do not offer blueprints, budgets, or programs. They only tease the listeners to begin to turn loose of the givens of the day and to live toward a new social possibility. The parables of Jesus clearly undermine the dominant social reality of his day. In fact, Jesus invites his listeners to a homecoming, for he insists that this kingdom is in fact one's true home. Every other place, no matter where, is a place of exile and alienation. That is why we know about "restless hearts" and "social unrest." These stories are an offer of genuine rest, at home.

3. The most compelling example of this imaginative articulation of an alternative in American culture may be in the liberated preaching of the black church. The best-known case, of course, is Martin Luther King, Jr. We ought not to miss the power of his language. He no doubt was a master politician and a social strategist and an adept manager of the media, but first and best, he had the tongue of a poet and the cadence of liberty in his speech. He was able to summon an exiled community out beyond the imperial definitions of the day which held his people in bondage. When he issued his famous poetic proposal, "I have a dream," that was just such a summons.[8] He did not have a concrete notion on how to enact that dream, but it was a beginning point of energy. The dream functioned as an act of incredible hope, but it was also an act of heavy critique which asserted that the present social reality is not working. It was an announcement that things would not stay as they were (cf. Isa. 43:18–19).

Out of the daring poetry of liberated black imagination, social reality began to crack open and homecoming became possible. The social reality that had seemed to be eternally ordained now appeared to be only a doubtful social contrivance. Second Isaiah's mockery of the gods serves the same end as did the dreaming of Martin Luther King, Jr. (cf. 41:21–29):

> The poetry of 2 Isaiah dreams of homecoming and begins to nullify Babylonian definitions of reality.

> The parables of Jesus initiate dreams of homecoming and begin to subvert the oppressive social institutions and presuppositions of his day.

> The oracles of Martin Luther King, Jr., dance about Stone Mountain and begin to cause trembling in the racist structures of the day.

All three of these poetic acts are models of liberated, liberating speech that stands in sharp contrast to our conventional domesticated speech. We mostly are scribes maintaining the order of the day. We mostly are appreciated by and paid by people who like it the way it is, who do not sense our exile and resist discerning it, who do not yearn for a homecoming because we have fooled ourselves into thinking this present arrangement is our home. To accommodate such social reality, our language becomes prosaic and didactic, because it helps keep the lid on things. Our language becomes descriptive, because it is better to tell *what is* than to trust *what will be*. Our church talk becomes dull and contained as all other talk in such a flat imperial society as ours.

Such a flattened tongue permits no vitality in ministry. Consider the phrase, "freedom of the pulpit." That phrase does not mean a license so that the minister can say any fool thing he or she wants. Rather it means that we are agreed that what is said here is to be said out of the power and freedom and affront of the gospel, without accommodating the conventions of the day. The pulpit—the speech practice of the church—is the place for imaginative speech that does not conform to the economic interests, moral limits, or epistemological convictions of the dominant culture.[9] Such speech is not imperative or exhortative or coercive. It tells no one what to do, but it redescribes the world so that Babylon, which looked so benign, is now seen as exile, so that Palestine, which was loved and lost, now looks like home, so that we who looked like docile slaves are on our way rejoicing. The central task of ministry is the formation of a community with an alternative, liberated imagination that has the courage and the freedom to act in a different vision and a different perception of reality.

Two reference points are available for such a new way of speech. On the one hand, the text and the tradition give us the materials for new metaphors. On the other hand, the present reality of pain energizes and illuminates the metaphors. The interaction of remembered text and present pain form the matrix out of which comes new speech. It is clear that 2 Isaiah's poetry is precisely such an interaction of text and pain.

## The Unfettered Power of the Word

Second Isaiah has remarkable things to say to his contemporaries that have no point of reference in domesticated reality. What he says is not derived from his Babylonian experience. His poetry is indeed about the powerful overriding word of God which will finally have its say in history (Isa. 40:6–8; 55:10–11). This theology of the word refers to a sense that there is an indefatigable agency at work in the historical process that takes its own free course and has its decisive say without conforming to the power and processes of the day. The God who is the subject of the word is also the subject of transformative action in the experience of Israel. The tradition of Isaiah in its early rootage had insisted that Yahweh's decree is more powerful than alien empires (cf. Isa. 14:24–27; 37:26–29). That word is rooted in God's primal intention, but it comes to fruition in concrete historical experience. As Yahweh had created the world by decree (Genesis 1; Ps. 33:4–9), so the history of the Near East and life of Israel begins again by that same speech.

Scholars have long noted that the poetry of 2 Isaiah is bounded by "the word." At the beginning in 40:8:

> The grass withers, the flower fades;
> but *the word of our God* will stand for ever.

The grass presumably refers to the pretensions of the Babylonian empire. That empire, contrary to appearances, is incredibly transitory and not to be feared or respected. The purpose of God will outlast the empire and all of its posturing (cf. the metaphor in Pss. 90:5–6; 103:15–16). At the conclusion of the corpus, the poet returns to the theme:

So shall *my word* be that goes forth from my mouth.
It shall not return to me empty,
but it shall accomplish that which I propose. (Isa. 55:11; au. trans.)

The promise of God over the historical process cannot be defeated.

The word of the word is utilized negatively concerning false gods who can speak no word. The lawsuit form of Isa. 44:22-23 taunts the other gods. They are challenged to speak: "tell us . . . tell us . . . declare . . . tell us." But there is a long silence in heaven, because the other gods are mute and dumb (cf. Isa. 44:18; Ps. 115:5-7). Speech is power. To have power, a god must speak. Such speech must be a serious decree that causes something to happen. But Babylonian gods are silent, have no word to speak, because they can cause nothing.

By contrast Yahweh is a God who speaks, whose word is effective and whose decree is carried out in the world. In 55:10-11, the speech of Yahweh is not futile. Yahweh does what Yahweh says (46:11). Yahweh must therefore be taken more seriously than the Babylonian gods. What Yahweh speaks is the fall of Babylon and the corresponding liberation of Israel. The same word that frees Israel is the word that creates worlds. Thus 55:12-13 envisions a transformation of creation, the inversion of Gen. 3:18. The word will transform both creation and imperial history. That speech permits Israel to go home.

That transformative word is an incredible promise asserted against the reality of the empire. God's way in the world may use Babylon (Jer. 25:9; 27:6), even as it used Assyria (Isa. 10:5-19), and subsequently will use Persia (Isa. 45:1). But the purposes of Yahweh are never controlled by the empire. Everything for this poet hinges on Yahweh's sovereign freedom, first to use Babylon, and then to dispose of Babylon, without regret or reservation. Yahweh uses and disposes of empires to work his decree in relation to this exiled people. The decree prevails. Empires come and go in relation to it. It is that sovereign word that comes to fleshly reality in the coming of Cyrus (44:24-28). It is the word (v. 26) which culminates in Cyrus (v. 28).

The contrast between the powerful purpose of God and the claims of the empire is articulated in the familiar words:

My plans are not your plans,
neither are your ways my ways, says the Lord,

For as the heavens are higher than the earth,
so are my ways higher than your ways,
and my plans than your plans. (Isa. 55:8-9; au. trans.)

This is not some kind of mysterious transcendentalism. It is rather a claim that purposes coming to realization are in fact the purposes of God and not those of Babylon (cf. 14:24-27). Indeed the voices of Babylonian power are mute and inconsequential (41:21-23, 26), not to be trusted or feared.

The claims of an overriding purpose from Yahweh will be difficult for us. We are all children of modernity. We take things as we see them. We do not credit easily the claims of poetry that are against the hardware of the day. It is hard to trust poetry more than custom hardware. That no doubt is a problem for us moderns, but it is not exclusively a modern problem. Every imperial agent wants to reduce what is possible to what is available.[10] No doubt this poetic insistence was difficult the first time it was uttered, because it was against the presumed data of the situation. The claim was not obvious then. It was only obvious to this poet who had uncommon, unfettered imagination. His capacity was to set in motion a new historical venture that changed the shape of Judah's history. But the change began in his liberated, imaginative speech about the overriding purpose of God in the process.

## Memories with a Future

Like Ezekiel before him, this poet is deeply rooted in the tradition.[11] Imagination is not a freelance, ad hoc operation that spins out novelty. Imagination, of the kind we are speaking, is a fresh, liberated return to the memory. When 2 Isaiah returns to the memory, he reads the tradition for his own moment, even as did Ezekiel for his. But because the situation is different, the anticipatory outcome of the tradition is also very different. Whereas Ezekiel read the memory as a statement of judgment and rebuke, 2 Isaiah reads it as a new gift. He does not regard the past as a closed record, but as a force that still keeps offering its gifts.

*Abraham and Sarah* (51:2-3) become a point of reference for the comfort of exiled Judah that are seen not to be without hope.[12]

*Barren Sarah* (54:1-3) becomes the fruitful mother of a whole new community. Her children, like those of the ancient midwives (Exod. 1:15-22), will outnumber the children of the empire.

*Noah* (54:9–11) becomes the model for the announcement of steadfast love, for the exile is like a chaotic flood and it is to end in peace and compassion.

*David* (55:3) becomes the root of a new covenant made to the whole community.[13] As David lived out of the promise, so the whole community can now live out of the promise.

To find in the memory such power for the present and for the future requires free sensitivity and intergenerational identity. It requires a break with the kind of imperial individualism that believes all the promises must be given to me, now. It takes courage to explore the memory, especially in a situation of amnesia like ours. Perhaps the community of the poet has no memory, for the empire insists that particularistic communities forget their particular rootage for the sake of universal myths. The particulars are such an embarrassment to the regime. People who believe the universal myths are easier to administer, for then we are all alike and indeed we are really replaceable parts. It is not different among us. When we have completely forgotten our past, we will absolutize the present and we will be like contented cows in Bashan who want nothing more than the best of today. People like that can never remember who they are, cannot remember their status as exiles or that home is somewhere else. It takes a powerful articulation of memory to maintain a sense of identity in the midst of exile.

## The Poet as Pastor

This poet operates with incredible pastoral sensitivity. He wants his community to think afresh, decide afresh, and act freely. He knows that this is a terrifying possibility. We are frightened nearly to death to run any risks, to stand out in the crowd, to go against conventional opinion. Who knows? If one criticizes the Babylonian arrangement, one might lose a job or a place in the university. The poet, for that reason, is present as a pastor, to nurture, nudge, and reassure about the little moves of liberated identity. Not many of us make big moves, only little moves. Even these scare us.

This nurturing of counterconsciousness is best expressed in the salvation oracles (41:8–14; 43:1–5; 44:1–4), which counter the fear and intimidation with a "fear not."[14] To utter the assurance is to recognize the fear. It is to read it as normal and without reprimand, but it is also to respond to it, to deal with it, to overcome it. The salvation oracle is an assurance of solidarity.

The form appears to have rootage in the old war traditions of Yahwism which assured Yahweh's presence with and commitment to Israel in the midst of military danger (cf. Exod. 14:13; Deut. 20:3-4). The form is used in this poetry to reassure exilic Israel that Yahweh's presence and solidarity with Israel more than offset the threat and reality of Babylon:

> Fear not, for I am with you,
> be not dismayed, for I am your God. (41:10)

> Fear not, you worm Jacob,
> you men of Israel!
> I will help you, says the Lord;
> your Redeemer is the Holy One of Israel. (41:14)

> Fear not, for I have redeemed you;
> I have called you by name, you are mine.
> When you pass through the waters
> I will be with you,
> and through the rivers, they shall not overwhelm you. (43:1-2)

When you pass through the waters, through the danger point, through the police station, through the customs office, when you are called to give an account of your new identity, you will not be there alone. The assurance, in the form it is cast in Isa. 43:1-5, is an announcement that sounds like a baptismal formula: "I have called you by name, you are mine." You belong to the hopes and memories of Yahwism. You do not belong to Babylon. You are mine, not theirs. Such a liturgical formula is not worth much unless it comes with an act of concrete solidarity, which presumably it did. This rhetorical act of solidarity is a life-changing assertion because it begins to dismantle the conventional assumption that Babylon is the only game in town. Think what kind of imagination it would take to envision and articulate an alternative identity! Such imagination is evident in the claim of salvation oracles in the midst of the empire. It is also evident in the claim of baptismal reassurance in the midst of an alien culture.

The intimate pastoral "fear not" is matched in this poetry by an imaginative assertion, no doubt acted out in liturgy, of the enthronement of Yahweh. The poet invites the community to a scenario in which the gods are on trial.

The other gods are invited to testify on their own behalf:

> Set forth your case, says the Lord;
> bring your proofs, says the King of Jacob.
> Let them bring them and tell us
> what is to happen.
> Tell us the former things, what they are,
> that we may consider them,
> that we may know their outcome;
> or declare to us the things to come.
> Tell us what is to come hereafter,
> that we may know that you are gods;
> do good, or do harm,
> that we may be dismayed and terrified. (41:21-23)

But of course they cannot:

> Behold, you are nothing,
> and your work is nought;
> an abomination is he who chooses you. (42:24)

The contrast is complete, for Yahweh can and does speak effectively.

> I stirred up one from the north, and he has come,
> from the rising of the sun, and he shall call on my name;
> he shall trample on rulers as on mortar,
> as the potter treads clay.
> Who declared it from the beginning, that we might know,
> and beforetime, that we might say, "He is right"?
> There was none who declared it, none who proclaimed,
> none who heard your words.
> I first have declared it to Zion,
> and I give to Jerusalem a herald of good tidings. (41:25-27)

Yahweh speaks because he has something to say about his powerful decrees that change historical reality. The function of this rhetoric is to contrast Yahweh and the gods, to distance Yahweh from imperial reality, to assert Yahweh's incomparability. But the theological intent is to delegitimate and dismiss the other gods, thereby overthrowing the imaginative, symbolic power of coercion practiced by the empire. By creating space for celebration of Yahweh, the poet creates space for liberated action. Freedom against Babylon is rooted in the liturgical assertion of Yahweh's unchallengeable governance.

The poet asserts the contrast in most absolute categories:

God is with you only, and there is no other,
no god besides him. (45:14)

To whom will you liken me and make me equal,
and compare me, that we may be alike? (46:5)

My glory I will not give to another. (48:11; cf. 42:8)

It is as though one were to juxtapose the God of the gospel with the gods of consumer capitalism, just as the old liturgy has contrasted the God of Moses and the gods of the Pharaoh (Exodus 5—10). The liturgy becomes a trial scene, in which each god is invited to give evidence of its authority, its power, its capacity to get things done, its ability to keep its promises.

The gods of Babylon have seemed so beyond reach, to be presumed and eternally taken for granted. But that is because no one had posed a serious question. Now this poet has the courage to ask, to look more closely, to inquire, "When was the last time a Babylonian god did anything that mattered for our well-being?" It turns out that the gods of the empire are a fraud, much noise and no substance, not able to make any difference at all. This other God, the one named in the tradition of Israel (Exod. 3:14), is shown by this poet to be the real one, the one with power to be trusted, even toward homecoming (45:21). Now again, notice the imaginative act of this remarkable poetry. Second Isaiah's reading of reality was not evident on the face of it. Jewish life in Babylon could have been read differently. It is an act of poetic courage that this poet is able to shape the perception of the community in a very special way, to read reality from the point of view of exile and homecoming, to reject every imperial reading. The outcome of the poetry—and it is only poetry and not a political proposal—is that the gods of Babylon are to be laughed at because they cannot in fact make any difference (41:21-24). Israel thus is freed to think differently about its own future and its loyalties. The competing loyalties that float around this community are named and assessed, the one to truth and validity, the other to falseness and emptiness. This partisan poetry stares the community in the face and waits. It requires a decision.

## New World Poetry

The authority for this staggering and subversive poetry that assaults the empire and creates space and courage for Israelite praxis is founded in the initial assertion of Isa. 40:1-11. This passage, frequently reckoned as a "call narrative," asserts the authority upon which the poetry is based.[15] The dialogue of that text concerns the commissioning of the poet by the divine council.[16] The poet portrays a conversation in the divine council that authorizes the poet to articulate an alternative vision of social reality (cf. 1 Kings 22:19-23).

The one commissioned is authorized to speak Yahweh's sovereign word of power, which is contrasted with the failed word of the empire: "the grassy empire withers, the word abides" (vv. 6-8).

In the face of pretenders to real power, Yahweh is asserted as the real king who must be acknowledged (v. 9; cf. 52:7). The formula, "behold your God," probably borrowed from the liturgy of enthronement, announces a new governance which destabilizes all would-be rulers.

On the basis of this alternative governance acted out in a liturgy of enthronement, the poet dares to announce the imperative, "comfort, comfort" (40:1).

To comfort genuinely hopeless people who have flattened futures is not an easy business. This kind of language functions as exile-ending speech. It is the announcement that homecoming is possible. But what does it mean to comfort? It does not mean to assure people it is all right to accept the imperial regime. If they wanted such an assurance, they would not have come to this poet. Rather, it means to give people permission to see the exile for what it is and to begin to move home.

The summons of this poet is not to express religious poetry. It is to shape communal imagination so that its true situation can be discerned. People cannot operate in new ways unless they are able to see afresh their real cultural circumstance. A new circumstance is brought vigorously to speech by this poet:

Israel is invited to sing a new song to celebrate a new regime. The new song is to replace the anthem of the empire (42:10).

This poetic speech debunks Babylonian gods and makes them objects of scorn (46:1-2).

This speech dismantles Babylonian power which had become autonomous (47).

This speech invites Israel to eat different bread (55:1-3), not the bread of the Herodians and the Pharisees (Mark 8:15), not the bread of the empire (cf. Daniel 1) which does not nourish, but new free bread.

Every aspect of this community is invited to a new orientation.

The new orientation wrought by poetry out of memory through liturgy consists in rereading reality through three metaphors:

*Exile* is a sense of not belonging, of being in an environment hostile to the values of this community and its vocation. Exile is practiced among those who refuse to accept and be assimilated in the new situation. Psalm 137 is a passionate resolve not to be assimilated. The poetry of 2 Isaiah in turn is a summons away from such assimilation.

*Babylon* refers to a concentration of power and value which is dominant and which is finally hostile to the covenant faith of this community. The empire regularly seeks to domesticate such a community with a special vocation and characteristically ends in oppression.

*Homecoming* is a dramatic decision to break with imperial rationality and to embrace a place called home where covenantal values have currency and credibility.

The juxtaposition of exile, Babylon, and homecoming means that this poetry of 2 Isaiah is not aimed simply at geographical, spatial possibility but at a relational, covenantal reality. The poetry permits a very different reading of social reality, opening up quite new social possibilities. The poetry evokes the sense that the world can and will be organized differently. Only a poet could make available such a drastically subversive conviction and invitation.

## NOTES

1. Most prominent is the work of Brevard Childs, *Introduction to the Old Testament as Scripture* (Philadelphia: Fortress Press, 1979), 325-38. See esp. the careful work of Ronald E. Clements, "The Unity of the Book of Isaiah," *Interpretation* 36 (1982): 117-29; and idem, "Beyond Tradition-History: Deutero-Isaianic Development of First Isaiah's Themes," *Journal for the Study of the Old Testament* 31 (1985): 95-113. See also Brueggemann, "Unity and Dynamic in the Isaiah Tradition," *Journal for the Study of the Old Testament* 29 (1984): 89-107.

2. Martin Luther, "The Babylonian Captivity of the Church," in *Three Treatises* (Philadelphia: Fortress Press, 1960), 115-260.

3. On the general field of the metaphor of exile, see Ralph Klein, *Israel in Exile: A Theological Interpretation* (Philadelphia: Fortress Press, 1979). On a contemporary use of the metaphor as it has been filtered through the Book of Revelation, see William Stringfellow, *An Ethic for Christians and Other Aliens in a Strange Land* (Waco, Tex.: Word Books, 1973).

4. I regard the two recent letters of the American Roman Catholic bishops concerning nuclear arms and economics as an indirect appeal to a situation of exile. In ever such a gentle way, the bishops have asserted that the church in America now lives in a context whose values are fundamentally in tension with the claims of the church's faith.

5. See my discussion of this function of poetry in the prophets in *The Prophetic Imagination* (Philadelphia: Fortress Press, 1978).

6. On the power of Jesus' stories to break and dismantle the dominant reality, see John Dominic Crossan, *The Dark Interval: Towards a Theology of Story* (Allen, Tex.: Argus Communications, 1975). Crossan's book reflects an important direction of scholarship, derived especially from the work of Amos Wilder and Paul Ricoeur.

7. Sallie McFague (*Metaphorical Theology: Models of God in Religious Language* [Philadelphia: Fortress Press, 1982]) has shown how the metaphor of "Kingdom of God" stands at the center of the biblical tradition and represents a threatening, inviting alternative of every kingdom "of this age."

8. On the capacity of King to use the old tradition in imaginative, poetic ways for the sake of the present, see James H. Smylie, "On Jesus, Pharaohs, and the Chosen People," *Interpretation* 24 (1970): 74–91.

9. On the cruciality of a universe of discourse, see Herbert Marcuse, *One-Dimensional Man* (Boston: Beacon Press, 1964), chap. 4. Stanley Hauerwas, in *A Community of Character* (Notre Dame: Univ. of Notre Dame Press, 1981), and in many of his works indicates this cruciality.

10. Karl Barth has insisted that one must begin with what is *real* and then work from there to what is *possible*. When the movement is inverted, as it is in most liberal theology, imperial definitions of what is possible are at the outset determinative of what is real.

11. The appeal to the tradition made by 2 Isaiah has been well documented by Bernhard Anderson: "Exodus Typology in Second Isaiah," in *Israel's Prophetic Heritage* (New York: Harper & Row, 1962), 177–95; idem, "Exodus and Covenant in Second Isaiah and Prophetic Tradition," in *Magnalia Dei, The Mighty Acts of God*, ed. F. M. Cross, W. E. Lemke, and P. D. Miller, Jr. (Garden City, N.Y.: Doubleday & Co., 1976), 339–60.

12. On this text, see Brueggemann, "Will Our Faith Have Children?" *Word and World* 3 (1983): 272–83.

13. See Otto Eissfeldt, "The Promises of Grace of David in Isaiah 55:1–5," in *Israel's Prophetic Heritage*, 196–207. Richard J. Clifford, "Isaiah 55: Invitation to a Feast," in *The Word of the Lord Shall Go Forth: Essays in Honor of David Noel Freedman in Celebration of His Sixtieth Birthday* (Winona Lake, Ind.: Eisenbrauns, 1983), 27–35, takes issue with Eissfeldt's thesis of democratization but shows in yet another way how the Davidic tradition serves as hope for the generation of exile.

14. For mapping of the form, see Claus Westermann, "The Way of the

Promise Through the Old Testament," in *The Old Testament and Christian Faith,* ed. B. W. Anderson (New York: Harper & Row, 1963), 200–224. See Westermann's more detailed analysis in "Sprache und Struktur der Prophetie Deuterojesajas," *Forschung am alten Testament* (Munich: Kaiser Verlag, 1964), 117–24. See the more recent discussion of Edgar W. Conrad, "The 'Fear Not' Oracles in Second Isaiah," *Vetus Testamentum* 34 (1984): 129–52; idem, *Fear Not Warrior,* Brown Judaic Studies 75 (Chico, Calif.: Scholars Press, 1985).

15. Frank M. Cross, "The Council of Yahweh in Second Isaiah," *Journal of Near Eastern Studies* 12 (1953): 274–77.

16. On the importance of the divine council, see Patrick D. Miller, Jr., *Genesis 1—11* (Sheffield: JSOT Press, 1978), chap. 1.

# 5

# Third Isaiah:
# The Theological Legacy of
# a Struggling Community

## PAUL D. HANSON

In critical biblical scholarship, chapters 56—66 of Isaiah generally are regarded as the product of disciples of Second Isaiah. This seems to be the most satisfactory way of explaining close thematic connections between chapters 40—55 and 56—66 on the one hand, and the unmistakable evidence of different historical and sociopolitical settings on the other. Accordingly, chapters 40—55, constituting the writings of the so-called Second Isaiah, are seen as words of promise, comfort, and encouragement to the Jews living in exile circa 550 B.C.E. Chapters 56—66 are taken as the words of some of those who, inspired by Second Isaiah and enabled by the Cyrus Edict of 538 B.C.E., actually made the return to the Jewish homeland.

The essential correctness of this literary theory is assumed in our discussion of Third Isaiah. We shall see, moreover, that the message of the writings in Isaiah 56—66 becomes intelligible precisely when seen against the background of the earlier promises found in Second Isaiah. Since a comprehensive demonstration of this assertion would go far beyond the confines of a single essay, we shall choose one image that runs through the Isaianic corpus by way of illustration. It will not be difficult to recognize how this approach involves issues related to the wider sixty-six-chapter corpus of Isaiah, the subject of the next chapter.

The image we choose is that of light and darkness. Within a community understanding reality within the stringently moral terms of a covenant relationship, the contrast between light and darkness takes its place alongside parallel contrasts like life and death, blessing and curse, salvation and judgment. Because Israel viewed the universe in moral terms, the quality of life experienced by the community was not due to blind fate or divine caprice. Light, life, blessing, and salvation were descriptive of a people living within a sound, healthy covenantal relationship. Darkness, death, curse, and judgment were the conditions afflicting those who had broken covenant.

We find the image of light and darkness used in two types of contexts with two different functions. In times of complacent optimism, moral laxity, and cultic apostasy, the prophets gave warning that the prosperity enjoyed by the people and the even more glorious times they anticipated were an illusion, for their repudiation of Yahweh's righteousness and compassion was leading them toward a harsh reversal. The contrast between light and darkness thus was invoked in words of indictment and warning of impending judgment. Amos, for example, spoke out against the unrighteous rich and powerful citizens of Israel during the reign of Jeroboam II in the following terms:

> Woe to you who desire the day of the Lord!
> Why would you have the day of the Lord?
> It is darkness, and not light. (Amos 5:18)

In a second type of context, the image of light and darkness was applied with quite the opposite force. Here the prophets faced not the problem of a populace arrogantly disdainful of the way of righteousness, but rather a sorrowing people, smarting under humiliating defeats, facing a frightful enemy and on the edge of despair. Such a people did not need further depiction of darkness and judgment and gloom. It already was engulfed by them. What it needed was a glimpse of hope beyond despair, of light piercing through the darkness.

In the Isaianic corpus, we find a splendid example of the image of light and darkness invoked to foster hope in words of the eighth-century prophet Isaiah (in other words, First Isaiah!) spoken during the Syro-Ephraimite crisis around 732 B.C.E. At that time the world seemed to be falling apart, with Judah situated at the heart of an international maelstrom. The Jewish state to the north had joined forces with Syria in a hostile military operation against Jerusalem. King Ahaz felt that there was no recourse save becoming a vassal of powerful Assyria. Isaiah was convinced that this was tantamount to a covenant with death. But right when the situation seemed most hopeless, and the people were on the brink of despair, the prophet was inspired to proclaim a remarkable divine word of hope to the afflicted and oppressed of his people:

> The people who walked in darkness
>   have seen a great light;
> those who dwelt in a land of deep darkness,
>   on them has light shined. (Isa. 9:2)

Isaiah's words of admonition and promise notwithstanding, the leaders and the people of Judah continued to flirt with false gods and fickle alliances, and over the course of the seventh century, threatening clouds were gathering. This process culminated in the single most devastating event of the entire history of ancient Israel, the Babylonian destruction of Jerusalem and the ensuing exile of the upper echelons of the population to a land where Marduk was worshiped as the supreme deity. The literature of the time reverberates with self-questioning and religious doubt. That Yahwism survived this crisis is in no small part due to the message of Second Isaiah. To people wondering whether Yahweh had forsaken them forever, Second Isaiah delivered an oracle of an imminent reversal of fortune:

> I will turn darkness before them into light,
>   the rough places into level ground. (Isa. 42:16b)

The beautifully poetic words of Second Isaiah are among the most inspiring of the entire Bible. Peering with holy imagination beyond appearances to the ultimate grounding of all reality in God, Second Isaiah was able to speak of glorious restoration and healing. He even named the Persian King Cyrus as the messiah who would be God's instrument in returning the exiles to their land, enabling them to rebuild their temple and community (Isa. 44:24—45:7).

A sizable number of the exiles were sufficiently inspired by the words of Second Isaiah to break with the security of their Babylonian habitat and, in what was described as a "second exodus," to travel the difficult road back to their homeland. Fully in the spirit and style of their prophetic leader, an anonymous poet captured the high hopes of the returnees in words again employing the image of light and darkness:

Arise, shine; for your light has come,
  and the glory of the Lord has risen upon you.
For behold, darkness shall cover the earth,
  and thick darkness the peoples;
but the Lord will arise upon you,
  and his glory will be seen upon you.
And nations shall come to your light,
  and kings to the brightness of your rising. (Isa. 60:1-3)

Here the image of light is turned up to its most radiant level. Its source is Israel's God, who has caused divine blessing to shine on a people whose glory is to be recognized by the nations and their rulers. For a people that had suffered so severely, this was truly an uplifting notion, one worthy of following with openness and affirmation.

What was in fact the experience of those who acted on Second Isaiah's brilliant promise? The bulk of Third Isaiah gives us a surprisingly full picture of that experience. But it is a shocking picture. A stinging prophetic word in Isaiah 59 will illustrate this corpus of literature and its bleak message. Once again we encounter the image of light and darkness:

We look for light, and behold, darkness,
  and for brightness, but we walk in gloom.
We grope for the wall like the blind,
  we grope like those who have no eyes;
we stumble at noon as in the twilight,
  among those in full vigor we are like dead persons. (Isa. 59:9b-10)

Those who returned with high hopes of divine restoration and blessing have collided with such bitter experiences as to best be described by taking the central Isaianic image of light and darkness and turning it rudely on its head: "We look for light, and behold, darkness!" What a shocking conclusion for people that had returned with hopes of being reconstituted as a holy people. Earlier they had eagerly greeted the divine promise, "Your people shall all be righteous; they shall possess the land for ever . . . you shall be called the priests of the Lord, people shall speak of you as the ministers of our God" (Isa. 60:21a; 61:6). They had looked forward to living in a city whose walls would be called "Salvation," and whose gates "Praise." This was to be a city in which justice was to be wedded with peace, and in which there would be equality and mutual caring. In Isaiah 59, we read of a situation that is diametrically the opposite:

> No one enters suit justly,
>     no one goes to law honestly;
> they rely on empty pleas, they speak lies,
>     they conceive mischief and bring forth iniquity . . .
> Their works are works of iniquity,
>     and deeds of violence are in their hands.
> Their feet run to evil
>     and they haste to shed innocent blood;
> their thoughts are thoughts of iniquity,
>     desolation and destruction are in their highways.
> The way of peace they know not,
>     and there is no justice in their paths;
> they have made their roads crooked,
>     no one who goes in them knows peace.
> Therefore justice is far from us,
>     and righteousness does not overtake us;
> we look for light, and behold, darkness,
>     and for brightness, but we walk in gloom . . .
> We look for justice, but there is none;
>     for salvation, but it is far from us. (Isa. 59:4–11)

The contrast with the promise of peace and justice found in Second Isaiah could not be drawn more sharply. We see not communal harmony radiating light and salvation outward to the rest of the world, but chaos, social anomie, and a collapse of political, economic, and judicial order:

> Justice is turned back,
>     and righteousness stands afar off;
> for truth has fallen in the public squares,
>     and uprightness cannot enter.
> Truth is lacking,
>     and the one who departs from evil becomes a prey. (Isa. 59:14–15)

What has led to this complete collapse of order and justice, right at a time when restored Israel seemed poised to assume a unique role in witnessing to divine shalom in the world as a Servant People? It would be folly to imagine that we could adequately answer this question, reaching as it does to the mysterious depths of human nature, as expressed so shockingly by Jeremiah: "The heart is deceitful above all things, and desperately corrupt; who can understand it?" (Jer. 17:9). But we do find hints in Isaiah 56—66 regarding the circumstances under which this negative turn occurred.

Politically, the Jewish community of the restoration period was one torn between two parties struggling for leadership and control. Ideologically and socioeconomically, they were different enough to lead to a deep polarization within the community. On the one side we find the leading priestly party, the Zadokites, advocating a hierarchical structure of community that assured their preeminence at the expense of the Levites and the followers of Second Isaiah whose writings are found in Isaiah 56—66. They demanded immediate rebuilding of the temple under their aegis, and the conformity of all elements of the community to their restoration program. One of their spokesmen, Haggai, proclaimed this divine command and promise: "Go up to the hills and bring wood and build the house, that I may take pleasure in it and that I may appear in my glory, says the Lord" (Hag. 1:8).

The other side saw matters quite differently. For reasons that are not altogether clear, but may be similar to the accusations leveled against the Zadokite priests in the Book of Malachi, the followers of Second Isaiah regarded the Zadokite temple as defiled and illegitimate. And they voiced their bitter opposition, again in the form of a divine oracle:

Thus says the Lord:
"Heaven is my throne
    and the earth is my footstool;
what is the house which you would build for me,
    and what is the place of my rest?
All these things my hand has made,
    and so all these things are mine . . .
But this is the one to whom I will look,
    the one that is humble and contrite in spirit,
    and trembles at my word." (Isa. 66:1-2)

The situation is a bleak one: Discord! Divided perception of divine will. Increasingly acrimonious confrontation between spiritual brothers and sisters, in which one side addresses the other thus:

You shall leave your name to my chosen for a curse,
    and the Lord God will slay you;
    but his servants he will call by a different name. (Isa. 65:15)

The Book of Isaiah, that book that is of such central importance to

Christian faith from the time of early disciples down to the present, thus ends on a very dark note. The last verse of Isaiah bluntly indicates this:

> And they shall go forth and look on the dead bodies of the men that have rebelled against me; for their worm shall not die, their fire shall not be quenched, and they shall be an abhorrence to all flesh. (Isa. 66:24)

This verse, and the somber tone that dominates the last eleven chapters of Isaiah, raise an important theological question, which we can again pose by focusing on the image of light and darkness. When we contrast the brilliant promises of light in Isa. 9:2; 42:16; and 60:1-3 with the bleak pictures of darkness and gloom in Isaiah 59, does the clash discredit the notion of divine promise to the suffering and the oppressed? Is a prophetic announcement of light breaking into darkness merely an opiate, an avenue of temporary escape from grim reality that substantially changes nothing? These are not questions to be answered glibly, at least not after the Holocaust of the Nazi period. But if we are cautious, I believe the writings of Third Isaiah, when contrasted with Second Isaiah, can offer some important insights.

The promises of Second Isaiah were not the facile promises of a utopian dreamer. Second Isaiah spoke of return with one eye on the divine Purposer and the other eye firmly fixed on the historical agent who would carry out God's plan for the return of the exiles, namely, the enlightened Persian monarch Cyrus. And he spoke of Israel's future role in the world economy in very specific terms, embellished to be sure with lavish symbolism and daring metaphors, but again clearly focused on a historical reality. Israel was to be present in the world as a servant people, as a people dedicated steadfastly to witness to God's standards of justice and peace by embodying justice and peace in its own life. Israel was to be present in the world for the well-being of the world, and in that way was to be more than self-serving, indeed (in the words of Isaiah 49), it was to be a light to the nations, that God's salvation might reach to the end of the earth.

I do not regard this as empty utopianism, but as a challenge extended to Israel to become the people God intended it to become, within a divine plan aimed at the restoration of the *entire* creation to justice and peace, or in a biblical terminology, to *šālôm*. Israel was to be a caretaker community, a vital nucleus in the larger cell, a community that, through undivided worship and wholehearted obedience, mediated divine reconciliation and healing to the whole human family.

That was the challenge of Second Isaiah. How did the people, once they had returned to the land, respond to it? We have already noted how they became locked in a bitter power struggle in which the vision of divine purpose and the prophetic word became a weapon aimed at discrediting and destroying the other side. Rather than becoming a nucleus of healing and restoration at the center of the nations, this community experienced the kind of sickness of soul that generates the darkest of human emotions and acts. This state of discord had a profound effect first on the way the two sides came to understand God's relation to the life of the Jewish community itself, and second on the way they came to view God's plan for the nations.

Internally, we see the conditions developing that have typically fomented apocalyptic movements. As one group sees its power to influence the social and political structures slipping away, and experiences deprivation and disenfranchisement, it quite naturally uses the symbols of its faith to envision imminent vindication in terms of God's direct intervention and ruthless judgment of the adversary party. After the series of stinging indictments and description of fallen order and justice that we read in Isaiah 59, the prophetic oracle goes on to envision a resolution of the problem as follows:

> The Lord saw it, and it displeased him
>> that there was no justice.
> He saw that there was no human,
>> and wondered that there was no one to intervene;
> then his own arm brought him victory,
>> and his righteousness upheld him.
> He put on righteousness as a breastplate,
>> and a helmet of salvation upon his head;
>> he put on garments of vengeance for clothing,
>> and wrapped himself in fury as a mantle.
> According to their deeds, so will he repay,
>> wrath to his adversaries, requital to his enemies;
>> to the coastlands he will render requital.
> So they shall fear the name of the Lord from the west,
>> and his glory from the rising of the sun;
> for he will come like a rushing stream,
>> which the wind of the Lord drives. (Isa. 59:15b–19)

This view of divine involvement in history is marked by a twofold contrast with the view of Second Isaiah: The human community is no longer a healing agent in the world, but is entirely passive; and the impact of God's presence on the world in general is understood not in terms of light and salvation, but of violent destruction.

A long salvation/judgment oracle in chapter 66 ends on a similar violent note:

> For behold, the Lord will come in fire,
>     and his chariots like the stormwind,
> to render his anger in fury,
>     and his rebuke with flames of fire.
> For by fire will the Lord execute judgment,
>     and his sword, upon all flesh;
>     and those slain by the Lord shall be many. (Isa. 66:15–16)

The universality of judgment in this oracle, again contrasting so sharply with the universality of divine salvation in Second Isaiah, leads to the second question, namely, what effect the sickness of soul of the community had on its attitude toward the nations. Though the question of the time of origin and authorship of the oracles against the nations is difficult to resolve, I believe it is significant that among the oracles of Third Isaiah we find a bloody, violent oracle against Edom that utilizes imagery and phraseology immediately reminiscent of the conclusion to chapter 59. After describing Yahweh marching back from his foreign campaign stained and dripping with blood, the oracle comes to this frenzied conclusion:

> I looked, but there was no one to help;
>     I was appalled, but there was no one to uphold;
> so my own arm brought me victory,
>     and my wrath upheld me.
> I trod down the peoples in my anger,
>     I made them drunk in my wrath,
>     and I poured out their lifeblood on the earth. (Isa. 63:5–6)

In reading such a violent passage, one cannot repress the question, What has come of Second Isaiah's magnanimous view of a servant people, patiently witnessing to God's šālôm and willing to suffer and even die for the reconciliation of humans with God? The answer that seems most plausible to me is this: The disharmony, acrimony, and hatred that tore into the heart of the people in the years after the return from exile created such an irrepressible sense of chaos as to lead to their projecting chaos onto the wider world. Yahweh was no longer seen as healer and redeemer, but as vengeful warrior who was about to "execute judgment . . . upon all flesh; and those slain by the Lord shall be many" (Isa. 66:16). In fact, those slain would be all those opposed to the protagonist party within Israel, and all the nations beyond, that is, all humanity except for the tiny remnant.

In trying to assess this grim chapter in late prophecy, and the many grim chapters that follow in later apocalyptic, I do not feel it helpful to resolve the problem by placing sole blame on the disaffected visionaries. Hurting apocalypticists are treated similarly today, and with equal injustice. For the fault lies not solely with those whose violent visions record their tortured experiences of an unjust, uncaring society and a threatening world, but with all those implicated in a situation like that of Isaiah 59 in which "truth is fallen in the public squares, and uprightness cannot enter."

In our society, as in that of the struggling community of Third Isaiah, the hopes and expectations of many are raised by glorious promises of prosperity, peace, and divine favor, only to be dashed on the rocks of poverty and marginalization. It is not uncommon for religious voices to join political ones in heightening such expectations while simultaneously being negligent in the demanding, often unspectacular task of working for justice and peace in society and world.

In a situation in which many are saying, peace, peace, when there is no peace, the legacy of the struggling community of Isaiah 56—66 can be received as a harsh but vitally important word of God. It comes to those of us who today are called to be God's people, a caretaker people mediating healing and reconciliation to a broken world by first embodying the justice and peace that lie at the heart of God's universal reign. In a political climate where people demand simple solutions that prove the other side totally wrong and their own side completely right, we are called upon to look beyond all political, social, and economic ideologies to the impartial justice and shared prosperity that arise from the presence in the world of a loving God. We may not like the rhetoric of militant blacks, strident feminists, revolutionary peasants, and radical pacifists, but in their apocalyptic pictures of impending judgment on structures of privilege and injustice we usually encounter a more accurate depiction of the life and death struggles occurring in our world than is given by those who would like to preserve the myth of manifest destiny and earned privilege. We err when our condescending ridicule of their images of conflagration and darkness leads us to overlook the moral indictment underlying their pessimism: "I looked, but there was no one to help; I was appalled, but there was no one to uphold." The apocalyptic picture is one in which structures of justice and peace have fallen because those with power to effect change no longer care about justice and peace, or suffer from an understanding of the issues of justice and peace totally distorted by greed and pride. The apocalyptic picture is not the illusion of a sick mind, but the moral dread arising in the face of a human dereliction that threatens all life on our planet.

In both of the spheres addressed so urgently by Third Isaiah, the domestic and the international, our world is staggering dangerously close to an abyss, the horrors of which we choose not to contemplate. One of the wobbly legs of this staggering world is called world hunger and poverty, the other nuclear politics. At a time when many people seem incapable of even engaging in reflection on these problems and potential solutions, so enormous and frightening are they, we must ask what responsibility the community of faith has.

Now as never before, it is our responsibility to be agents of healing and reconciliation as a worshiping community embodying God's justice, compassion, and peace in the world. We are called to be a nucleus of health in a sick world as a means of witnessing to God's alternative to the darkness of nuclear winter and the deathmask of starvation. But what if this nucleus is ravaged by disharmony, parochial striving, and distrust? The salt loses its taste, the lamp on the hill is covered, the people of God become the people of this world.

I have observed two patterns emerging among communities of faith that have lost their sense of being servants in the world for the sake of the well-being and peace of the whole world. On the one side is the pattern commonly adopted by ultraconservative and fundamentalistic churches, according to which communities slip into a narrow sectarian mentality issuing forth in condemnation of all rivals within the household of faith as well as condemnation of all the peoples of the world. The death wish of Hal Lindsay can serve as a case in point. More common to our experience, perhaps, is the liberal tendency, namely, that of denouncing apocalyptic pessimism as crude and deviant, and clothing reality with a far more promising aura. In relation to the former pattern, I believe it is our responsibility to bear witness to the central theme of Scripture that God's loving concern embraces all peoples, indeed all creation. The whole creation is thus our calling. In relation to the latter, I believe we must be honest interpreters of the modern situation who eschew not only the death-wish mentality but also illusory optimism. In unmasking the unreality of both, we must point to the basis for peace and justice in a truly troubled world that is grounded in reconciliation with life's Source.

I shall close by giving an example of the type of witness that I believe we are called to give in relation to one specific issue, nuclear politics. Already in the days immediately following the first testing of the atomic bomb and the first military deployment of this dread weapon, two responses emerged, that of blind optimism predicated on ultimate faith in the goodness and creative genius of humanity, the other of prophetic realism and admonition.

First, our example of illusory optimism is taken from William L. Laurence's book, *Men and Atoms*:

> This great iridescent cloud and its mushroom top, I found myself thinking as I watched, is actually a protective umbrella that will forever shield mankind everywhere against the threat of annihilation in any atomic war.
>
> The rising supersun seemed to me the symbol of the dawn of a new era in which any sizable war had become impossible; for no aggressor could start a war without the certainty of absolute and swift annihilation.
>
> This world-covering, protective umbrella, I have since become convinced, will continue shielding us everywhere until the time comes, as come it must, when mankind will be able to beat atomic swords into plowshares, harnessing the vast power of the hydrogen in the world's oceans to bring in an era of prosperity such as the world has never even dared dream about.

Second, our example of prophetic realism and admonition is taken from the reflections of Albert Einstein:

> As scientists, . . . we dare not slacken in our efforts to make the peoples of the world, and especially their governments, aware of the unspeakable disaster they are certain to provoke unless they change their attitude toward one another and recognize their responsibility in shaping a safe

future. . . . The war [World War II] is won, but peace is not. The great powers, united in war, have become divided over peace settlements. The peoples of the world were promised freedom from fear; but the fact is that fear among nations has increased enormously since the end of the war. The world was promised freedom from want; but vast areas of the world face starvation, while elsewhere people live in abundance. The nations of the world were promised liberty and justice; but even now we are witnessing the sad spectacle of armies of "liberation" firing on peoples who demand political independence and social equality. . . . Territorial conflicts and power politics, obsolete as these purposes of national policy may be, still prevail over the essential requirements of human welfare and justice. . . . The prognosis for our postwar world is not bright. The world situation calls for bold action, for a radical change in our approach and our political concepts. Otherwise, our civilization is doomed.

There is truth in the dread visions of the apocalyptic seers among us, as there was in the time of Third Isaiah. Our world is sorely threatened by human cruelty, prejudice, greed, distrust, and idolatry. But there is an inestimably greater truth in the apocalyptic event that arises above all others—the event on the cross, in which both the tragedy that lies at the center of human existence and the hope that lies beyond tragedy were embraced and offered to all peoples. In the darkness and light of the cross, we are called to be God's servants in the world, servants neither deluded by utopian illusions nor paralyzed by pessimistic dread, but mediating the justice and peace and reconciliation that we have experienced in Christ and that we seek to embody in a life of innercommunal harmony for the sake of God's world.

# 6

# Isaiah 1—66:
# Making Sense of
# the Whole

## CHRISTOPHER R. SEITZ

### Preliminary: A Methodological Note

I want to term the approach adopted in this study of Isaiah "Canonical Critical."[1] "Canonical" emphasizes the role the Book of Isaiah plays as Scripture for the present community of faith (as context and control for interpretation). One further implication of the term "canonical" is that the intention of the final shape of the Book of Isaiah, while difficult to perceive, is greater than the sum of all previous intentions of the text, as these have been reconstructed in modern historical analysis.[2] By "critical" I wish to acknowledge my indebtedness to historical analysis (my own prior reading), which seeks to locate the text at prior historical moments. The intention of the final form of the Book of Isaiah need not be unavailable to those who have first seen the text "deconstructed" through historical analysis.

### Introduction

My topic, "Isaiah 1—66: Making Sense of the Whole,"[3] can be focused by asking two key questions: (1) What is the source of the Book of Isaiah's unity? (2) How are we as readers to make sense of Isaiah as a sixty-six-chapter whole? Though related, these are two slightly different questions. The source of the Book of Isaiah's disunity[4] and the nature of its present unification are theories about the book that developed externally, through critical method and conjecture. Many argue, for example, that the present unity of the book was achieved on a sociological level: disciples saw to it that three separate collections were made into one.[5] A decision external to the text caused its present unification. The question of Isaiah's literary coherence for us as readers—what is the sense of the whole book?—is a different one, an internal one. Are clues given to us as readers and hearers of the Word of God presented in Isaiah that enable us to make sense of its sixty-six-chapter shape? As has been made clear in Isaiah research of the past century, these sixty-six chapters can be critically divided into three separate blocks of material. But is there an internal, reader-oriented movement across the sixty-six-chapter length and breadth that we can perceive and that enables us to hear, see, and stand before this entire *ḥazôn yeša' yāhû*, this "vision of Isaiah" (1:1), as the book calls itself? Are we even entitled to expect such internal coherence? Or must we work with the present critical theory, and divide in order to conquer?

The language "divide and conquer" is not chosen by accident. Modern critical theory assumes a distance between the text and reader. The way we as hearers and readers of God's Word are to understand that word and participate in the story is normally illustrated by a process of analogy. How is my situation like that related in the story? But the process of analogy is more complicated in Isaiah because of the sheer size of the book and its three-century historical backdrop. So critical theory posits three separate prophetic figures, with three separate prophetic words, spoken to three separate historical audiences: one in Judah in the Assyrian period; one in Babylon in the Babylonian period; one in Judah in the Persian period, in order to give the reader a clearer point of standing. We are then to find our place in relationship to the Word of God by aligning ourselves with the various characters in the story: we are the stubborn Ahaz, or the unproductive vineyard, or the haughty women of Jerusalem, or the despondent exiled community, or rigid hierarchical priests of the postexilic period, or visionary prophetic figures who stand in need of no temple.[6]

I simplify the critical procedure in order to make a point. Critical division of Isaiah simply aids in breaking up the book against more or less plausible historical backdrops. Our problem as readers in Isaiah is compounded because, with its sheer size, the book gives us so many options and possible points of standing. At least with Israel's shorter prophetic books, once the historical distance was understood and over-come, we had fewer choices about where to stand. Not so with Isaiah. In this essay I am not interested in engaging in an extended critique of modern historical analysis, nor in showing how a clairvoyant Isaiah wrote the whole book in the eighth century. What I want to do is challenge three leading tenets of modern critical theory. I do this not because I think historical analysis is bankrupt, but because it remains one essential (preliminary/heuristic) way among many to enter into the world of the text.[7] In the five preceding chapters, we have participated in the deconstruction of the Book of Isaiah. This disciplined look at "Three Isaiahs" forms an essential part of our work on the Book of Isaiah as a whole. At crucial points, however, historical deconstruction threatens to blunt or obscure several key internal features that have been supplied to help us hear the Word of God across and including all sixty-six chapters. What I offer, then, is not a complex new literary theory. I hope that by demonstrating something of the Book of Isaiah's own efforts at unity and coherence, I might make our point of standing, as preachers, readers, and hearers of the Word of God in Isaiah, more stable and coherent.

The three tenets of recent historical analysis I want to challenge are these: (1) That the final shape of the book is accidental or the result of successive phases of supplementation, phases more independent than integrative. Hence our ability to talk about 1, 2, 3 Isaiah as separate books and even separate folk (see 3). (2) That in the present shape of Isaiah we move in clear geographical terms from Judah to Babylon, and then back to Judah; and in clear temporal terms, from eighth through seventh to sixth centuries B.C.E. This movement happens when we cross internal boundaries marked at chapters 39/40 and 55/56. (3) That internal division is necessitated because we move from a clear proto-Isaiah prophet to a Babylonian prophet to a Persian prophet.[8] All three of these leading tenets are interconnected in the present 1, 2, 3 Isaiah model for interpretation. Before looking at them individually and in detail, I will illustrate something of their force by propounding a *māšāl*.

## The *Māšāl* of the Farmhouse

When the prophet Ezekiel wanted to clarify Israel's situation before Yahweh, he occasionally used the *māšāl*. The *māšāl* illustrates through comparison and contrast. The New Testament counterpart is the figure or parable ("The Kingdom of God is like . . . "). This *māšāl* wants to get at the question of just what the Book of Isaiah is like. I trust my *māšāl* will not become a *ḥîdāh*, a riddle—Ezekiel's other favorite device— which hides more than it gives away.

I once lived in an old single-story farmhouse in the North Carolina countryside. One of the many interesting things about the house was its construction. From the outside it had a standard rectangular form that seemed in no way unusual. But the years and the weather revealed a secret the external form had hidden. Upon entering the central hall, it was clear that the right side of the house had settled more than the left. Further investigation indicated that a main portion of a rear interior wall was actually covered with exterior siding. In fact, there was even a full sash window in the original building, facing out onto the interior space. Deduction: three or more houses had been combined to form our farmhouse.

Critical scholarship has reached similar conclusions about the Book of Isaiah. The result is the 1, 2, 3 Isaiah theory. But the rooms in the Isaiah house have not been looked at closely enough, and here the example from the *māšāl* is helpful. From the outside, my farmhouse had a distinct unity of form. This suggested that the growth of the house took place with an eye toward its final shape. Other alternatives were possible for construction, namely, the house could have grown without organic, or external, unity, because its final form was the result of the merger of various small and separate houses. However—and this is an important point the *māšāl* helps illustrate—when we examined the interior of the farmhouse, we learned that the growth of the house took place only with reference to the original building. Several separate houses, each with an independent life, had not been merged. If such had been the case, we would have seen a far more unusual external form, one that would reveal three originally distinct shapes now merged together. And far more internal confusion would also have resulted—hallways would not necessarily connect. Who would need three kitchens, or three bathrooms, in strange and unneeded proximity? But more than external unity had been achieved in our farmhouse. The additions to the house had forced modifications on the original building (though that odd sash window remained!), modifications so concerned with the internal logic of the expanded house that the original structure, not to mention the additions themselves, could no longer function as coherent independent buildings. In sum: The finished house was more *one* than *three*.

Critics were right to spot a certain unwieldiness in form in the Book of Isaiah—more so perhaps than in my farmhouse. This is why three divisions were made. Internally, it *is* difficult to get from room to room in Isaiah. This must be admitted. But this difficulty may not be so overwhelming as the present critical theory suggests—that, standing in one section of the house, we cannot move to another room without exiting altogether and then entering the new section by its own external door. Let us turn to the first leading tenet, that the Book of Isaiah is a collection of three independent books, to explore the interior of the house further.

### Three Independent Collections?

The notion of three independent collections has already been challenged by readers on several grounds.[9] Let me point out three of the more obvious objections:

1. There is only one superscription, or opening rubric, for the entire collection. This superscription calls the whole book a "vision of Isaiah which he saw concerning Judah and Jerusalem," during the reigns of four kings of the eighth and seventh centuries (Isa. 1:1).

2. There is only one narrative telling of the commissioning of a prophet in the book (i.e., Isaiah, in chap. 6). Though it has been argued that a call-narrative exists for the so-called Second Isaiah in Isaiah 40, a close reading of chapter 40 shows this to be unlikely (I will return to this question below). One suspects special pleading and the solving of a problem created by the critical method itself: one searches for a prophetic figure required by the critical theory and then finds one. No one even attempts to sketch out the call narrative of a Trito-Isaiah.

3. The literary boundaries between 1, 2, 3 Isaiah are not marked in any special way. The reader confronts a new tone and emphasis moving across the border of Isaiah 39/40, but the transition from 55 to 56 is no more cumbersome than others within so-called First Isaiah. For example, the movement from Isaiah 12 to the oracles against the nations in chapters 13—24 is far more noteworthy, and may flag as much or more reader interest as other trans-Isaianic crossings.

In all three cases (one superscription, one call narrative, no clear literary boundaries), it has been argued that original marks of the three independent collections were dropped out when they were fused into one. But this is far from obvious. Isaiah 40—55 has a highly structured organization that gives no evidence of the loss of an original call narrative or superscription. And Isaiah 56—66 has always shown itself resistant to independence, despite arguments from sections of the critical guild.[10] Moreover, even if one argued for original independence, one would have to explain why clues that originally stressed the threefold independence have now been removed.

Pursuing this question a bit further, we see that an opposite tack has been taken in the development of Isaiah tradition. In Isaiah 40—55, six references to the "former" and "latter things" key us as readers to the message and themes of earlier chapters: the words of judgment spoken in the Assyrian period are the "former things," to be contrasted with words of comfort in the exilic period (41:22; 42:9; 43:9; 43:18; 46:9; 48:3). "Behold, the former things have come to pass, and new things I now declare; before they spring forth I tell you of them" (42:9); "Remember not the former things, nor consider the things of old. Behold I am doing a new thing" (43:18-19).[11] The "servant" (s.) figure of Isaiah 40—55, not developed in Isaiah 1—39, is however picked up in Isaiah 56—66. The "servant" has become the "servants" of the restoration community: "I will bring forth descendants from Jacob, and from Judah inheritors of my mountains; my chosen shall inherit it, and my servants shall dwell there" (65:9; see also 56:6; 63:17; 65:8, 9, 13, 14, 15; 66:14). These links with the prior traditions of the book are established *from within* the new material itself. They are not artificially imposed on an expanded and therefore incoherent text. But there is still other evidence that an eye toward meaningful construction informed the process of growth within the Book of Isaiah.

Situated at the very end of the "First Isaiah" material, chapters 36—39 occupy a pivotal position in the Book of Isaiah.[12] These chapters form a unified narrative set in the period of Hezekiah. They are almost an exact duplicate to the narrative from 2 Kings 18—20.[13] Now there is very little evidence of this kind of historical chronicle anywhere else in Isaiah 1—39, nor such a clear example of direct literary borrowing within the book. So we are moved to ask why this section appears where it does, and what it is trying to say. Its central burden is the announcement that the Assyrians had failed to capture the sacred Jerusalem, despite the bravado speeches of Assyrian siege troops in the region. Though its message is a positive one from the standpoint of one living in Jerusalem, "He [Sennacherib] shall not come into this city, for I will defend this city to save it" (37:33-35), it creates a potential problem for the reader and the flow of the book. If the Assyrians fail to capture Jerusalem, and bring an end to Judahite independence, what do we make of Yahweh's words of judgment against Israel spoken earlier in the book? Why would words of comfort to Jerusalem need follow in Isaiah 40:1-2 if Jerusalem had not fallen? The pivotal chapter 39 answers this question. It understands that Yahweh had spared Jerusalem, Hezekiah, Isaiah, and the inhabitants of Zion in the Assyrian period—but it tells of darker days ahead, days when the Assyrians will be upstaged by the Babylonians, who will overrun Jerusalem and exile the population. A theological problem and a readership problem are solved in one fell swoop by the inclusion of chapters 36—39. God's word of judgment over Israel's sins, declared in the Assyrian period by Isaiah, is to be fulfilled in the Babylonian period. At the same time, the reader is prepared for the words of comfort that appear in Isaiah 40ff., words that only make sense once the sentence of judgment, the "time of service" of Isa. 40:2, has been carried out.

In sketching out the function of Isaiah 36—39, another problem in the theory of independent books is uncovered. Isaiah 36—39 has its own literary prehistory and has only found its place in so-called First Isaiah due to the introduction of new levels of tradition. In my judgment, this is the most telling problem in the 1, 2, 3 Isaiah theory. So-called Second and Third Isaiah are far more coherent and temporally locate-able than First Isaiah, which has its own complex history, extending in some cases into a much later time period. The whole notion of Second and Third Isaiah depends in no small part on there being a clear First Isaiah. Such an Isaiah is not to be found. Isaiah 1—39 is an extremely complex collection of material, with a diverse background (witness chaps. 36—39).[14]

Without adding to the list of direct citations, I will focus the First Isaiah problem as I did with Isaiah 36—39. One of the historical problems of the Book of Isaiah takes its most obvious form in Isaiah 1—39: How do a prophet and language of judgment tied to the Assyrian period now function in a book that moves well beyond the time frame of the Assyrian threat? More specifically, did words of judgment, related to the Assyrian threat, not come to fruition, since the Assyrians failed to capture Jerusalem and themselves disappeared from history shortly thereafter? The book answers this question by showing the Assyrians to be just one of many foreign nations sent by Yahweh for judgment. In the oracles concerning foreign nations (chaps. 13—23), Babylon now heads the list of those countries sent forth by Yahweh for judgment against his own people (Isa. 13:1-22). There is widespread agreement that this oracle found its place in so-called First Isaiah only after the historical Isaiah had passed from the scene.[15] More to the point, the oracle concerning Babylon in Isaiah 13—14 now works in conjunction with a theology of history embracing the whole book, and not just so-called First Isaiah.

Discussion of this question moves us to the second tenet of critical theory related to 1, 2, 3 Isaiah, that of the temporal and geographical movement of the book.

## Temporal and Geographical Movement

There is no doubt whatsoever that, in its final form, the Book of Isaiah moves from the Assyrian, through the Babylonian, into the Persian period. Or, from the mid-eighth century (Isaiah's call, circa 742 B.C.E.), through the seventh (rise of the Babylonians in 612 B.C.E.), into the sixth (exile and restoration, 597 through 530s). I have just tried to show, for example, how the period of the seventh century was collapsed in Isaiah 36—39 to move us into the sixth century, Israel in exile, and Isaiah 40—55.

One of the things that the 1, 2, 3 theory stresses is that this chronological movement corresponds to the literary movement from 1—39 to 40—55 to 56—66: Proto-Isaiah and Assyria; Deutero-Isaiah and Babylon; Trito-Isaiah and Persia. But again, the most telling objection to this schema is to be seen in so-called First Isaiah. Although there is evidence for temporal rearrangement and movement well beyond the Assyrian period throughout chapters 1—39, the problem can be most easily focused in the opening chapter of the book. It will be helpful to look at the contents of Isaiah 1 more closely.[16]

Isaiah 1:1-9 establishes the audience of the divine word as a nation already "sinful" (1:4), already unsure of its master's crib (1:3), already "laden with iniquity" (1:4). Not only are they rebellious, they "continue to rebel" and "still are smitten" (1:5), even though their "country lies desolate" (1:7), "aliens devour their land" (1:7), and the city of Jerusalem is left as a "booth in a vineyard." "If Yahweh of hosts had not left us a few survivors," an unknown voice confesses, "we should have been like Sodom and Gomorrah" (1:9).

The perspective of the opening chapter is comprehensive in scope. We enter the world of Isaiah in the middle of things, well into the story of Yahweh and Israel. Cities have already fallen. Already only Zion is left. Already a people has revealed a choice for disobedience and lack of trust. Already we have moved well beyond the eighth century, and the threat of Assyrian invasion, and nearly into the seventh, when the threat had become a reality. The most obvious historical background for these allusions is the one again set forth in chapters 36—39. When was Zion left like a booth in a vineyard? During the invasion reported in Isaiah 36—37.[17] Isaiah 38—39 revealed that Zion was magnificently spared, and then it hinted at darker days ahead. Note the movement in Isa. 1:10–26. The fact of Zion's sparing is recognized to be a warning, not a matter of rejoicing. Zion continues to present vain offerings (v. 11), and is enjoined to "stop evil, begin good, seek justice, correct oppression" (v. 17). Though God is willing to "reason together" (v. 18), we learn in 1:21 that the option for rebellion (v. 20) was chosen. "The faithful city became as a harlot" (v. 21), leading to God's own judgment, "I will turn my hand against you" (v. 25), and "afterward you will be called . . . the faithful city" (v. 26).

In Isaiah 1, then, the entire literary, historical, and theological sweep of the whole Book of Isaiah is reviewed. Here the Book of Isaiah reveals its own internal, temporal logic, one related to Yahweh's journey with Israel, the nations, and the cosmos itself. From our standpoint as readers, we are given a perspective *right at the beginning* that God alone can see. We do not have to wait to cross 2 and 3 Isaiah boundaries to know the whole story. I want to return to the effect this has on us as readers in a moment. Five distinct phases are revealed in the broader book, and they are sketched out here: (1) judgment over Israel/Judah in the Assyrian period; (2) judgment over Zion/Judah/Jerusalem in the Babylonian period; (3) judgment over Israel's neighbors; (4) judgment over the whole cosmos; (5) restoration of Zion and a new creation. The fifth phase is picked up in the oracle of 2:1-5: "It shall come to pass in the latter days that the mountain of the house of the Lord shall be established as the highest of the mountains."[18] It is also hinted at throughout Isaiah 1—12 with the same words: "and it shall come to pass" or similar expressions—"in that day" or "in the latter days" (2:1, 11, 12, 20; 3:18; 4:2; 6:18, 20, 21, 23; 9:1; 10:20, 27; 11:10, 11; 12:1, 3). That is to say: days ahead, following the judgment, days of Zion's restoration and international shalom. Chapter 12 resounds with the theme of Zion's future redemption, and the links to 2 and 3 Isaiah are obvious. So too, judgment over Israel in the Assyrian period, spoken of by the eighth-century Isaiah in language of the Day of Yahweh, is used to foreshadow a yet greater Day of Yahweh, involving a judgment over all the nations of the earth and the cosmos itself (2:20-22).[19] Only after this judgment will the glorious restoration ensue.

This fivefold pattern of Yahweh's plan for Israel, the nations, and the cosmos does not coordinate easily with 1, 2, 3 Isaiah partitioning. The judgment over the nations, hinted at throughout Isaiah 1—12, is made explicit already in Isaiah 13—23, followed by the cleansing of the cosmos itself in Isaiah 24—27—sections still in so-called First Isaiah. Though the judgment, exile, and restoration of Israel is sketched in the movement from 1 to 2 to 3 Isaiah, First Isaiah already explores this pattern in the context of God's fuller plan for creation. Similarly, themes of restoration are not delayed until the triumphal 2 Isaiah; they are presented within the context of God's larger plan, as early as Isa. 2:1-5, and as late as Isaiah 60—62.

One of the major themes of restoration within so-called First Isaiah is that focused on a remnant that survives in Zion, takes root, and represents the seeds of future hope. This image can be seen at various points in the first thirty-nine chapters. Subtly: "Zion shall be redeemed by justice, and those who repent in her, by righteousness" (1:27). And more boldly:

In that day the branch of the Lord shall be beautiful and glorious, and the fruit of the land shall be the pride and glory of the survivors of Israel. And he who is left in Zion and remains in Jerusalem will be called holy, every one who has been recorded for life in Jerusalem, when the Lord shall have washed away the filth of the daughters of Zion and cleansed the bloodstains of Jerusalem from its midst by a spirit of judgment and by a spirit of burning. Then the Lord will create over the whole site of

Mount Zion and over her assemblies a cloud by day, and smoke and the shining of flaming fire by night; for over all the glory there will be a canopy and a pavilion. It will be for a shade by day from the heat, and for a refuge and a shelter from the storm and rain. (Isa. 4:2-6)

Recall as well Isaiah's response to God when the vision of judgment is revealed to him in Isaiah 6: "Then I said, 'How long, O Lord?' And he said, 'Until cities lie waste . . . and the land is utterly desolate. And the tenth that remains in it shall be burned again, like a terebinth or an oak whose stump remains standing when it is felled. The Holy seed is its stump'" (6:11-12; au. trans.).

This focus on Zion is not dropped, as one might expect, once we enter Second Isaiah. One of the direct implications of the 1, 2, 3 Isaiah theory is that the reader must shift from a Jerusalem perspective in First Isaiah to a Babylonian perspective in Second Isaiah, with a return to Jerusalem in Trito-Isaiah. This geographical displacement is forced upon the reader, it is claimed, when one crosses the boundary at Isaiah 40, territory of the great prophet of the exile. There are several reasons this view of the matter overstates the literary evidence.

1. The opening words of comfort in Isaiah 40, which God commands be proclaimed, are not to be proclaimed to exiles, but to Jerusalem: "Comfort, comfort my people," says your God, "Speak to the *heart of Jerusalem*, and cry to her . . ." (40:2). The herald of good tidings is to get up on a high mountain (40:9). Not in Babylon—this is a herald of good tidings *to Zion*.[20]

2. In my judgment, the figure of the servant introduced in these chapters is in fact the exiled Israel, so some geographical movement away from Judah is recognizable to the reader. This movement is anticipated to a degree within so-called First Isaiah. The depiction of exile as one form of God's judgment, to be reversed when the period of judgment is completed, is mentioned at several points in Isaiah 1—39 (11:10-11; 14:1-4; 27:12-13; 39:5-8, anticipating chaps. 40—55). However, the focus on Zion/Jerusalem, even desolated in the coming period of judgment (chaps. 1—12), is not done away with when the exilic fate is brought into more prominence in Isaiah 40—55. The mission of the servant does not take place in isolation from the fate of Zion/Jerusalem (see especially 49:14—50:3; 51:1-3; 51:12—52:12; 54:1-17).

3. Related to this, Zion/Jerusalem is the clear object of interest in

Isaiah 49—55, the second half of Second Isaiah. She is the afflicted, storm-tossed one, who stands in need of comfort: "For the Lord will comfort Zion; he will comfort all her waste places" (51:3); "Awake, awake, put on your strength, O Zion; put on your beautiful garments, O Jerusalem, the Holy City" (52:1). In my judgment it is Zion who confesses the saving activity of the servant on her behalf, in the controversial fourth servant poem (52:13—53:12).[21] The work of the servant (52:13—53:12) means Zion can again sing with joy: "Sing, O barren one, who did not bear; break forth into singing and cry aloud" (54:1).

As readers of Isaiah 1—39 we are prepared for this sentence of judgment which has so obviously fallen upon Zion, the barren one who has not borne. And we are also ready for Zion's restoration, as foretold as early as Isa. 2:1-5. Language related to Zion's restoration is maintained beyond the boundary of Isaiah 55. We see this same language appearing in Isaiah 60—62: the longed-for fulfillment of God's plan of restoration. In sum, while the image of exile and return has a clear place in so-called 2/3 Isaiah, this is not the only perspective the vision of Isaiah seeks to develop there. The central focus remains on the judgment and restoration of Zion, and this focus is upheld even in the so-called prophecies of the exile. The ultimate target of restoration remains, finally, the whole created order.

### The Prophetic Persona in Isaiah

One possibility for understanding the unity of the Book of Isaiah would be to say that it focuses on one person, the prophet Isaiah. But this is far from obvious. It is precisely because the book explodes beyond the historical bounds suggested in the superscription (Uzziah to Hezekiah) that we are not moved to trace all sixty-six chapters back to an Isaiah who did in fact live during the reigns of these Judahite kings. Here the 1, 2, 3 theory seems to be on firm ground. The mention of the name Cyrus at 45:1, the highly probable Babylonian-period background of chapters 40—55, the quite plausible Persian-period origin of chapters 56—66 all point to the relative success of the 1, 2, 3 theory. But this success is only relative, insofar as it points out obvious problems in trying to defend Isaianic authorship of all sixty-six chapters. The puzzle as to the unity of the Book of Isaiah is indeed related to the question of the prophetic persona developed, or not developed, in the book. But here the 1, 2, 3 theory does not adequately address the problem.

There is another more obvious literary reason why seeking the unity of the book around the person—or author—Isaiah is implausible. Isaiah is startlingly absent not just from 2 and 3 Isaiah collections—he does not put in much of an appearance in First Isaiah, the collection attributed to him. The significance of this fact must also be explored in any discussion of the unity of the book.

From the standpoint of the full form of the Book of Isaiah, the reader notes how very little attempt is made to render a reasonable portrait of the prophet Isaiah beyond chapter 39. Put another way, not only do we see nothing of a new (Second) Isaiah in chapters 40—55, we see nothing of the prophet First Isaiah either. The same is true of Isaiah 56—66. In other words, no attempt has been made by secondary hands who filled out the original Isaiah oracles to convince the reader that material (chapters 40—66) unlikely to have emerged from the period spoken of in the superscription (eighth century) did in fact come from First Isaiah. We read on into these new sections of the book with absolutely no attempt being made to depict Isaiah at work in their pages. As a matter of fact, to echo our earlier statement, there is even within those chapters attributed to First Isaiah very little in the way of third-person accounts relating Isaiah's movements, actions, and speech. How does the Book of Isaiah function with such a flexible, if not elusive, presentation of the prophet?

Now it should be admitted that it is partly due to the peculiar nature of biblical—or more restrictedly—prophetic narrative that we have a difficult or incomplete view of the prophet qua prophet. Isaiah does not step boldly forward to identify himself as the author, narrator, and main actor in the chapters that follow. We are used to this kind of narrative, for we find it in much modern literature. *Moby Dick,* for example, opens with words from the first-person narrator, "Call me Ishmael," and for the moment it matters little to the reader whether this Ishmael is the author Herman Melville or not. He tells the tale. He writes the words. And he is a trustworthy teller precisely because he is a character in the story as well. The same is not true of the Book of Isaiah.

In order to get some perspective on this, merely turn to the opening verses. The book is called a "vision of Isaiah." But Isaiah does not tell us this. Someone else describes to us that what we are about to read is a vision of Isaiah. Immediately upon entering the world of the vision (1:2), we confront not the person of Isaiah nor even the speech of Isaiah, but the speech of God. The entire first chapter makes absolutely clear that it is direct speech of God. The prophet and prophetic mediation of divine speech remain hidden from our view.[22] Even in chapter 2, where we are again informed that what follows is from Isaiah (2:1), the person of the prophet is nowhere to be found. We have to wait until chapter 6 for the prophet to step boldly before our eyes: "In the year that King Uzziah died, I saw the Lord . . . " (6:1).

These chapters (6—8), brief though they are, make the attempt to show us something of Isaiah, just as Ishmael takes up a role in *Moby Dick*, along with presenting his own speech and that of others to the reader. In this "Isaiah Memoir," as it is often called, the prophet Isaiah acts as spokesman for Yahweh, as we assume he is in chapters 1—5. But he also acts as spokesman for himself. He emerges as a main character in the story, in confrontation with Ahaz, as awestruck receiver of God's call in the temple, as frustrated prophet whose word is not heard, as father of children with strange and symbolic names.

It might be better to compare the Book of Isaiah with another narrative style from modern literature, Ernest Hemingway's *The Old Man and the Sea*. In this story, the narrator never reveals his place in the tale he tells. The story is not about the person telling it. As a matter of fact, we accept as a reasonable fiction the narrator's ability to relate a tale without telling us who he or she is in the tale itself. At this point we might say the narrator is Hemingway, and we would be correct. But this does not get at the technique involved, which is more like that employed in the Book of Isaiah. This technique allows the narrator to remain hidden in order that the focus might fall on the tale itself, namely, a story about an old man, a young boy, and the sea.

In a similar way we might argue that the Book of Isaiah is not about Isaiah any more than *The Old Man and the Sea* is about its unknown narrator. Again, we would be closer to the truth but might miss what was in fact distinctive about Isaiah 1—66. Unlike *The Old Man and the Sea*, Isaiah does have a role to play, albeit a minor one (especially chapters 6—8; 36—39). The superscription of the book, and its attribution to Isaiah, lead us to expect that we will see something of the prophet, his speech, and his ways—both as narrator and as subject of the book. Like *The Old Man and the Sea*, however, the Book of Isaiah has a unifying subjèct that stands only in loose connection to its theoretical narrator, the prophet Isaiah, after whom the book is named. But before I say more about who or what the subject is, I want to draw one further contrast between Isaiah and another type of literature—this time within the biblical material itself.

It might be argued that in the above I have begun to put my finger on what is distinctive about Israel's prophetic literature. It might also be said that I was not the first to do so! In other words, I am telling no new tale about Israel's prophetic books, but am only pointing out what makes them different than some forms of modern literature or certain expectations we have about forms of narrative as different as the bylined *New York Times* article or the romance novel we see at the grocery checkout counter. But now I want to make some distinctions within Israel's own prophetic canon that I hope will move us closer to identifying the unique work that is the Book of Isaiah.

One might begin by saying that the problem with identifying the prophetic figures in the collections attributed to them is that they speak for God and therefore are sometimes lost behind the words they deliver.[23] This goes a long way toward the truth. But many of Israel's prophetic books tell us far more about their respective prophetic figures than the Book of Isaiah tells us about Isaiah. Both Ezekiel and Jeremiah give us ample room to see the prophetic mediator at work. Even a short work like Amos reveals interesting details about who Amos was: herdsman; dresser of sycamore trees; not a professional *nabi';* two years after an earthquake; in confrontation with priests at Bethel. In Hosea, it would be fair to say that the marriage of the prophet (chapters 1—3), allegory or real event, forms the interpretive cornerstone of the whole book.[24] Interest in prophetic figures, as well as speech identified as God's very own, has some precedent in Israel's prophetic books.

The best example of this, and noteworthy because of its historical proximity to the composition of the Book of Isaiah, is the Book of Jeremiah. There was at one time a very strongly defended theory about the development of the Book of Jeremiah (maintained in hybrid form today) that also argued for a threefold development—instead of 1, 2, 3 Jeremiah, however, one spoke about A/B/C Jeremiah.[25] A was traceable to

Jeremiah as direct (first-person) speech from him. B was composed of narratives about Jeremiah, that is, indirect speech (third-person), sometimes attributed to Baruch, a scribal assistant. C was from another hand still, but it too remained interested in the figure of Jeremiah, even when it was characterized as a pious distorting or deuteronomistic manipulation of him. Critics did not talk about 1, 2, 3 Jeremiah in the same sense as they described 1, 2, 3 Isaiah because A/B/C Jeremiah were, unlike 1, 2, 3 Isaiah, homogenized levels of tradition. That is to say, they were all mixed up together; they were not successive sections of the book, on the pattern of Isaiah.

Here is the major point where Jeremiah and Isaiah are so different: All three levels of Jeremiah tradition are concerned with the figure of the prophet Jeremiah. In fact, level B is often classified Biography. New tradition is generated in Jeremiah just as surely as original Isaiah tradition gave rise to a massive sixty-six-chapter book. But unlike 2 and 3 Isaiah, all new levels of Jeremiah tradition keep the prophet firmly in their sights. Jeremiah remains the main character in the fifty-two-chapter story.

I have already said that attempts to pull a prophetic figure out of 2 Isaiah have proven difficult, and out of 3 Isaiah, nearly impossible. The reason for this, in my judgment, is the concern within new levels of tradition to coordinate themselves with the old, the "former things." Development of separate prophetic personae would obviously aggravate this coordination. It could be argued that this is guarded against in Jeremiah by weaving the new tradition right alongside the old, so as to cause no reader confusion when new material is introduced.

I want to return to the observation I made earlier that divides yet more strongly the Jeremiah and Isaiah traditions. Not only is Isaiah strikingly, and logically, absent from 2 and 3 Isaiah, but he is virtually absent from so-called First Isaiah. Put another way, not only are Deutero-Isaiah and Trito-Isaiah elusive, but so too is Proto-Isaiah, Isaiah of Jerusalem, First Isaiah, or whatever you would call him. This makes Isaiah as a full book, or even as a reduced third, unlike not just Jeremiah, but also unlike the Book of Ezekiel, another prophetic book of equal length. The prophets Ezekiel and Jeremiah are introduced in the opening chapters of their collections, and they remain central figures throughout. Of shorter prophetic books, Amos and Hosea give us more information about their prophetic figures than does an even greatly reduced First Isaiah about

Isaiah. Recall that we see nothing of the prophet until chapters 6—8. The call narratives for Ezekiel (chap. 1) and Jeremiah (chap. 1) are the first encounters we have with the books attributed to them. As such, the prophetic mediation of the divine word is stressed. But in the Book of Isaiah, God does most of the talking. This is just as true in First Isaiah as it is in so-called 2 and 3 Isaiah. This "retraction of the prophetic persona" permits the Book of Isaiah to grow as it does without causing obvious readership problems. This feature of the Book of Isaiah also allows the subject of the story—God—to overshadow so completely the prophetic mediator or narrative voice. This feature makes the Book of Isaiah distinctive among the major prophetic books. This feature is maintained across all critically determined internal boundaries.

Related to this last observation, one final point can be made. The two places where the prophet Isaiah appears are in chapters 6—8, during the reign of Ahaz, and again in chapters 36—39, during the reign of Hezekiah. I have already noted the importance of chapters 36—39 in the larger flow of the book. Let me make another observation, related to the person of the prophet in these chapters. The superscription of the book (1:1) made it clear that the prophet Isaiah functioned during the reigns of four Judahite kings, Uzziah through Hezekiah. In chapter 39, in order to prepare for the replacement of Assyria by Babylon, the death of Hezekiah is envisioned. Do we not also have here an obvious statement about the prophet Isaiah? Namely, that he too will not live to see the Babylonian onslaught?

Though it has never been noted, so far as I know, this passing away of Isaiah as a (subtle) theme of chapter 39 may directiy inform the following chapter, the opening chapter of so-called Second Isaiah. Here God speaks to an unknown audience. Anonymous voices respond (vv. 3, 6)—the first positively; the second imperatively; the third questioningly. In the chapters that follow we see the search for a prophetic mediator (see especially 41:25-29), and God's selection and commissioning of the servant (see 42:1-4; 43:8-13). That is to say, in Second Isaiah a readership problem (where is the prophet Isaiah?) and a theological problem (who will speak for Yahweh in a new day beyond the "former things"?) are taken up and addressed in God's commissioning of servant Israel.[26] But this does not happen in such a way to remove an emphasis distinctly Isaianic. Just as God functioned in First Isaiah chapters as direct speaker, so he speaks directly in 2 Isaiah—over one hundred times in the first person. Even the choice of servant as mediator to Zion and witness to the nations does not mean that God steps to the side. He remains the most direct voice to address Israel, servant, Zion, in the whole book.[27]

## Conclusions

With these observations in place about the retraction of a prophetic figure in the Book of Isaiah, I am ready to draw some conclusions.

The Book of Isaiah is a book whose main character is God. This must be said at the outset, in order to clarify how Isaiah is distinctive over against Jeremiah or Ezekiel, where God shares far more of the stage with prophetic figures. God's dialogue in Isaiah is not primarily with a prophetic figure (Isaiah) or with prophetic successors (the servant; servants), though these take up very important roles. God's dialogue is with Israel and the cosmos, God's entire created order. In the book, the second major character alongside God is Zion. Zion functions as the concrete expression of God's dwelling with his creation.

With these observations in place, it might be fitting to call the Book of Isaiah "The Drama of God and Zion." In this drama, *chronos,* concern with linear time and the unfolding of the drama, is not done away with, but it is also not slavishly maintained. God reveals himself in a healthy Zion to his prophet Isaiah. God stands by Zion, to protect it. But Zion's welfare is threatened because of Israel's lack of attention to God, God's dwelling place, and his fuller plan for creation. The vineyard becomes a place of bloodshed and a cry. God himself brings a judgment upon Zion, his own place of intersection with his creation (chapters 1—12). In so doing, the whole created order is wracked (chapters 13—23; "Behold, the Lord will lay waste the earth and make it desolate, and he will twist its surface and scatter its inhabitants": 24:1). Zion is spared, but then it too falls (chapters 36—39). But through the suffering and the commissioning of the exiled servant, Zion is restored again (chapters 40—55). Zion sings out thanksgiving. The drama of God and Zion unfolds as we walk through the chapters, all sixty-six, of the Book of Isaiah.

We as readers are given a privileged point of standing in this drama. (Here is where *chronos* is subtly subverted.) Unlike Israel, the nations, Isaiah, or the servant, we as readers are privileged to see the whole journey in a twinkling in the opening chapters. Our point of standing prepares us for what is ahead. Much of the same technique is employed in the Gospel of Mark, where we as readers are shown who Jesus is from God's point of standing at his baptism, in the opening chapter (1:9), even while the characters in the story must wrestle and learn the difficult truth that this is the Son of God.[28] Their journey is a difficult one because they must discover by risk and by failure, forced to see the kingship of Jesus in realms that include suffering and death.

Our vantage point in the Book of Isaiah is a privilege and a responsibility. We know God's full intention for Zion early on (Isa. 2:1-5). But the final chapter of the Isaiah drama has not been written. More so than for the other prophetic collections, Isaiah remains open to the future, and it is doubtless for this reason that Isaiah is the most frequently cited Old Testament prophet in the New Testament. The church proclaimed that the trajectory of Messiah, so prominent in the Isaiah corpus, had reached its culmination in Jesus of Nazareth (Matt. 1:22 // Isa. 7:14). But the full restoration of Zion and the cosmos is never accomplished within Isaiah's own literary framework. So too, it remains a lively hope in the New Testament precisely because of the entrance into history of the one proclaimed Christ. The reign of the righteous Davidic scion was to usher in the eschatological age of peace and proper justice (Isa. 9:2-7; Isa. 11:6-9). This vision of Isaiah remains God's final will and purpose for the created order, a will and purpose not so much completed in Jesus Christ as sharpened and held out to the present community of faith, both in challenge and in promise.

The eschatological force of the whole Book of Isaiah cannot be described or contained by simple appeal to original historical setting. This force is obvious during the period of eschatological fervor represented by the literary section that concludes Isaiah (chaps. 56—66). But it is also established from the very beginning in the Isaiah drama. It remains the "vision of Isaiah which he saw" and in that sense is to be our vision as well, as we seek to hear and proclaim the promise of God in light of God's action in Jesus Christ.

## NOTES

1. The term is not without problems. See the discussion of James Sanders, *Canon and Community* (Philadelphia: Fortress Press, 1984), 21ff. Also, Brevard Childs, *Introduction to the Old Testament as Scripture* (Philadelphia:

Fortress Press, 1979), 69–83; James Barr, *Holy Scripture: Canon, Authority, Criticism* (Philadelphia: Westminster Press, 1983); Childs's review of Barr's work appears in *Interpretation* 38 (1984): 66–70.

2. A better term than "final form" is "full form" or "macro form." Canonical criticism is not the first methodology to stress the final or present form of the text—compare premodern interpretation. As employed by Childs (*Introduction to the Old Testament*), and in contrast to much premodern interpretation, analysis of "canonical form" emphasizes the *full form*, that is, the form the text takes after various constituent parts, revealed in critical analysis, are brought into final coordination, the result being the text as we now have it (sixty-six chapters of Isaiah). Observations about "full form" only follow once one has, through historical analysis, seen the constituent or multilayered quality of the biblical text, a quality occasionally noted but not viewed with the same exegetical significance in the premodern period.

3. For important background discussion, the reader should consult: Ronald E. Clements, "The Unity of the Book of Isaiah," *Interpretation* 36 (1982):117–29; idem, *Isaiah and the Deliverance of Jerusalem,* JSOTSS 13 (Sheffield: JSOT Press, 1980), 90ff; idem, "Beyond Tradition-Criticism: Deutero-Isaianic Development of First Isaiah's Themes," *JSOT* 31 (1985): 95–113; Childs, *Introduction to the Old Testament*, 316–38; Rolf Rendtorff, *The Old Testament: An Introduction* (Philadelphia: Fortress Press, 1986), 198–200; Walter Brueggemann, "Unity and Dynamic in the Isaiah Tradition," *JSOT* 29 (1984): 89–107.

4. Though suggested earlier as an aid for interpreting chapters 40—55, Bernhard Duhm focused the problem of literary disunity in his 1892 Handkommentar zum Alten Testament on Isaiah.

5. See, e.g., D.R. Jones, "The Traditio of the Oracles of Isaiah of Jerusalem," *Zeitschrift für die alttestamentliche Wissenschaft* 67 (1955): 226–46; J. Schreiner, "Das Buch jesajanischer Schule," in J. Schreiner, ed., *Wort und Botschaft* (1967): 143–62.

6. It might be said that the greater the historical specificity, the greater the potential for reader confusion . . . not in terms of understanding what the word meant or how it emerged, but in knowing how to relate to the present text as guide for faith and practice.

7. Exposing what Paul Ricoeur calls the "background" of a text.

8. Appeal to a "prophetic guild" behind 2 and 3 Isaiah reminds us that problems exist. In my judgment, terms like "The Prophet of Consolation," "Isaiah of Jerusalem," "The Great Prophet of the Exile," "Trito-Isaiah," or any other suggestions for fully independent prophetic personae within the book are terribly misleading. They are at best artificial or heuristic constructs, and at worst, insurers of disunity in the sixty-six-chapter corpus.

9. See the comments of Childs, *Introduction to the Old Testament*, 325ff; Rendtorff, *Old Testament*, 198–200.

10. If something was lost in Third Isaiah, we might hope that it was more than an original call narrative or superscription. In many respects, chapters 56—66 remain the most difficult section of the book to interpret on the basis of clear historical-critical findings.

11. For a full discussion, see Childs (*Introduction to the Old Testament*, 325-38) and Clements ("Unity of the Book of Isaiah," 117-29). Compare A. Bentzen, "On the Ideas of 'the old' and 'the new' in Deutero-Isaiah," *Studia Theologica* 1 (1948-49): 183-87; C.R. North, "The 'Former Things' and the 'New Things' in Deutero-Isaiah," in *Studies in Old Testament Prophecy*, ed. H.H. Rowley (New York: Charles Scribner's Sons, 1950), 111-26.

12. For important observations on Isaiah 36—39, see Peter Ackroyd, "An Interpretation of the Babylonian Exile: A Study of 2 Kings 20, Isaiah 38—39," *Scottish Journal of Theology* 27 (1974): 329-52; Ronald Clements, "The Prophecies of Isaiah and the Fall of Jerusalem in 587 B.C.," *Vetus Testamentum* 30 (1980): 421-36.

13. Isa. 36:1—39:8 // 2 Kings 18:13—20:19 (excepting Isa. 38:9-20).

14. See Ronald Clements (*Isaiah 1—39*, New Century Bible [London: Marshall, Morgan & Scott, 1980]) for a survey of recent theories of the growth of "First Isaiah." Also Rendtorff, *Old Testament*, 190-93. The following works must be taken into account: Herrmann Barth, *Die Jesaja-Worte in der Josiazeit* (Wissenschaftliche Monographien zum Alten und Neuen Testament 48 [Neukirchen-Vluyn: Neukirchener, 1977]); J. Vermeylen, *Du prophète Isaïe à l'apocalyptique*, 2 vols (Paris: J. Gabalda, 1977); Otto Kaiser, *Isaiah 1—12* (Old Testament Library 2d rewritten ed. [Philadelphia: Westminster Press, 1984]). These studies suggest a complex growth internal to chapters 1—39, apart from questions regarding the date and provenance of so-called Second and Third Isaiah. They demand a complete rethinking of the relatively simple formulation 1, 2, 3 Isaiah.

15. See Clements, *Isaiah 1—39*, 129-31.

16. For background discussion, see G. Fohrer, "Jesaja 1 als Zusammenfassung der Verkündigung Jesajas," *Zeitschrift für die alttestamentliche Wissenschaft* 74 (1962): 251-68; Childs, *Introduction to the Old Testament*, 330-33.

17. Or, for readers aware of the whole book: during the events of the fall of Jerusalem a hundred years later (597-587 B.C.E.).

18. Whether this famous pericope is "Isaianic," that is, original Isaiah proclamation, is a question of only relative importance in the context of this study. The same is true of other statements in Isaiah 1—12 concerning the future. They may well have emerged as Isaiah proclamation, during the specific events of the eighth century. What is of present interest is the effect the positioning of individual speech units, be they Isaianic or otherwise, has on the reader sensitive to the whole sixty-six-chapter flow of the book. When one succeeds in determining the historicity of a passage, the context for interpretation as pro-

vided in the specific literary arrangement of the present text itself may go unnoticed. The context for interpretation then becomes only the reconstructed historical circumstances which may or may not have given rise to the speech unit.

19. Clements, *Isaiah 1—39*, 46.

20. Claus Westermann (*Isaiah 40—66* [Philadelphia: Westminster Press, 1977] 43-44) defends the reading preferred in the RSV: "Zion, herald of good tidings." Zion/Jerusalem is apparently to speak words of comfort and encouragement to "the cities of Judah" (40:9). Though I find this reading less likely within the larger context of 40:1-11 and chapters 40—55, the point remains the same: 2 Isaiah maintains a focus on Zion/Jerusalem that was already developed in Isaiah 1—39.

21. This would have to be established through careful exegetical analysis of the place of the servant hymns in the overall structure of Isaiah 40—55, a task that lies outside the scope of this study on the whole Book of Isaiah.

22. In real contrast to the way we enter the Books of Jeremiah and Ezekiel (see Jer. 1:4-19; Ezek. 1:1-28).

23. Moreover, in time the prophet can become overshadowed by the literature that preserved the divine word for future generations (Zech. 1:5-6). The divine word was seen as more decisive than interest in the prophetic mediator as such.

24. The same cannot be said of the significance of Isaiah 6—8 for the sixty-six-chapter book.

25. See S. Mowinckel, *Zur Komposition des Buches Jeremia* (Kristiania, 1914).

26. Isa. 41:27-28: "I give to Jerusalem a herald of good tidings/But when I look there is no one/among these there is no counselor/who, when I ask, gives an answer. . . ." Isa. 42:1ff: "Behold my servant, whom I uphold/my chosen, in whom my soul delights/I have put my Spirit upon him. . . ."

27. The Targums, sensitive to the canonical flow of the sixty-six-chapter book, and sensing something of the retraction of the prophetic figure, supply a plural prophetic body who hear and respond to God's word. This group appears, for example, in 40:1: "The prophets prophesy words of comfort to Jerusalem." But they also appear throughout the sixty-six-chapter book, as often in so-called First Isaiah as in Second and Third Isaiah.

28. This perspective on the Gospel of Mark was emphasized by Jack Kingsbury in a lecture series on Mark, Spring 1985, at the Lutheran Theological Seminary at Philadelphia.